GOD AS A GARDENER

GOD AS A GARDENER

Exploring plants in Bible parables

DR. CAROLYN A. ROTH

MARIA LIN, ILLUSTRATOR

TATE PUBLISHING
AND ENTERPRISES, LLC

Published by Tate Publishing & Enterprises, LLC
127 E. Trade Center Terrace | Mustang, Oklahoma 73064 USA
1.888.361.9473 | www.tatepublishing.com

Tate Publishing is committed to excellence in the publishing industry. The company reflects the philosophy established by the founders, based on Psalm 68:11,
"The Lord gave the word and great was the company of those who published it."

Book design copyright © 2016 by Tate Publishing, LLC. All rights reserved.
Cover design by Samson Lim
Interior design by Jake Muelle

Published in the United States of America

ISBN: 978-1-68352-270-6
1. Religion / Biblical Reference / General
2. Gardening / General
16.07.08

To my husband, Bruce Roth

Acknowledgements

The following individuals provided advice and support in the preparation of this book:

Bruce Roth, my husband, edited the manuscript and double checked every Bible reference.

Maria Lin, the illustrator, who is a joy to work with.

Dr. Ed Bez, President of the Biblical Botanical Garden Society-USA, for encouragement and endorsement

Dr. Gerald McDermott, Anglican Chair of Divinity, History and Doctrine at the Beeson School of Divinity, for his ongoing encouragement and endorsement.

Tate Publishing Enterprise, particularly Stacy Baker.

Contents

Why a Bible Study About Parables Illustrated by Plants

God is infinite; he is eternal, everywhere, all knowing, and all powerful. In contrast, mankind lives a short life, i.e., eighty years. We are in a single place at any point in time. We don't know everything there is to know, and we are relatively powerless. Despite the differences between God and mankind, God wants to communicate with us. In scores of Old and New Testament parables, God used plants to illustrate his nature, spiritual truths about his kingdom, and how he wants us to live.

Interpreting Bible parables and plants in them isn't easy; twenty-first century society is far removed in time and culture from the Bible's original audience. The distance isn't only chronological, but social, political, and religious. Westernized individuals live in an industrial and technology-driven society. Often contact with plants grown for food is second or third hand. Individuals don't have an "aha" moment where they understand a parable by its comparison to a plant, such as a fig tree, grapevine, or thistle. To appreciate some parables, individuals need insights into plant life, what the plant looks like, how it grows, and how ancient people used it. We need to know how a plant's characteristics made it an appropriate, even optimal, illustration of God's character and will.

The good news is that basic plant characteristics—at least for most Bible plants—are fairly stable. The stability helps interpret plants in Bible parables. This book centers on twenty-four parables illustrated by plants. I researched these parables and plants to learn why God chose each plant to illuminate the parable's spiritual truth. Because Old and New Testament parables have different characteristics, I divided the book into a section on Old

Testament and a section on New Testament parables. Often the same plants were used in Old Testament and New Testament parables. That's because Christ and other New Testament writers borrowed heavily from Old Testament parables and illustrations.

The book is written for the average church member, rather than for seminarians and clergy. It's for individuals who want a different type of Bible study and those who love plants. This latter group may be individuals who want to grow plants in their home garden or in a church garden. They may be master gardeners or members of garden or nature clubs. Answering study questions, integrated into each chapter, deepens our walk with God. Questions can be pondered alone or discussed with friends in a Bible study group.

Each chapter contains a photograph of an original water-colored illustration of the plant(s). Most Bible plants were identified by Jewish rabbis, historians, and Israeli botanists. When I cited specific plant names, I relied on opinions of Michael Zohary, professor of Botany at the Hebrew University of Jerusalem, and of Nogah Hareuveni, creator of Neot Kedumim, the Biblical Landscape Reserve in Israel. The appendix provides information for individuals who want to grow parable plants.

Origins and Purpose of Bible Parables

When Christians think about parables, their minds default to Jesus's parables in the New Testament; however, parables didn't originate with him. Parables are scattered throughout the Old Testament. Seminarians and theologians debate what is and isn't a Bible parable. Often they deconstruct Bible allegories, metaphors, similes, and fables to determine if each meets criteria for a parable. In contrast to these worthwhile efforts, in this book a parable is a comparison where an image borrowed from the visible world is accompanied by a truth about the spiritual world.

Parables go back to antiquity. In the ancient Middle East, parables were a common method of teaching. They have the following characteristics:

- Attract our attention. We want to know the punch line or end point of the story.

- Stir up or excite us. Often, we remember a parable when other Bible content or a sermon is forgotten.

- Stimulate us to think. We ponder and discuss a parable to understand its meaning. By studying parables, we teach ourselves.

- Inform our opinions. As we add life experiences and mature, we understand and apply parables at differing depths.

- Preserve truth. For example, when we recall the parable of the wheat and the tares, we understand that when Jesus comes the second time, the righteous and unrighteous will be separated.

In both the Old and New Testaments, God's spiritual truths were often illustrated using plants. Ancient peoples lived close to the land and nature. They depended on plants for food, both for themselves and for their livestock. They grew plants in gardens and farms, i.e., herbs, grains, and grapes. Because ancient people understood plants, they readily interpreted parables illustrated by them.

A single parable doesn't teach the entire Bible or gospel. It teaches a single point. The first step in understanding the point is to read the entire parable. Don't rush to judgment or conclude immediately that you understand its point. Remember, it's God's divine being and will that we interpret in a parable, not our own preferences. Second, study a parable's context. Review what happened before the parable was told (back story). Know what occurred subsequent, or after, the parable was given (outcome). The back story and outcome both aid parable interpretation. Third, although individual parts of the parable develop its truth, not every part contributes to its meaning. Some parts of a parable are there to make the story flow or make it easier to remember. For example, in the parable of the ten virgins, the number of virgins with olive oil lamps may not impact the parable's interpretation.

Although a parable has one primary interpretation, it can have many applications. When we apply a parable, we put it into practical use in our lives. Application is personal. My husband and I interpret a parable the same way, but we apply it differently. Bruce's application reflects his work as a skilled craftsman, while my application is to the church Bible garden.

Section I

Plants in Old Testament Parables

The closest word to parable in the Hebrew language is *mâshâl*.[1] *Mâshâl* translates: to resemble, become like, and compare. In a parable, Jewish writers compared the visible (physical) world to the spiritual world; they used common, every day, visible occurrences to make their point about a spiritual truth. That's one reason ancient writers often used plants in their parables.

The exact number of Old Testament parables is debated. One scholar identified as few as ten, while another identified as many as twenty-six parables. Often scholars hold Old Testament parables to the same standard as those spoken by Jesus. They seem to forget or ignore that Israelite customs and language differed between Old and New Testament times. Further, Jesus was the son of God. Of course his words and actions were superior to those of man.

In Old Testament parables, readers learn about the moral and social life in different periods in Israel's history. We see agricultural practices and religious conditions across time. Old Testament parables attract us by their truth about life. They show man as he was, not as an idealized model. Old Testament parables were spoken, seen in visions, or acted out by a cast of characters to include prophets, priests, kings, and an orphaned son. Many were focused locally (Samaria, Jerusalem) and related to a particular event; however, others had national focus, like those of Isaiah and Ezekiel. Several Old Testament parables were fables where plants spoke; others were beautifully crafted poems.

While studying Old Testament parables, I noticed two features which weren't common in Jesus's parables. First, some parables didn't stand alone; they included another action. For example, Jotham's parable included a curse, while King Jehoash's included a warning. Second, many Old Testament parables were interpreted or explained through actions or outcomes in the same Bible chapter or subsequent Bible chapters. Only rarely was a parable's interpretation left to listeners or readers. Whether interpretations were or weren't provided, ancient listeners knew that they were to apply the parable to their lives.

The twelve parables reviewed in the successive chapters in this section aren't an exhaustive list of Old Testament parables illustrated with plants. Some parables were excluded because both the plant and the message were discussed in another parable, i.e., four in the book of Ezekiel and one in the book of Daniel were omitted because the plant appeared previously.

Reference

1. Strong, James. *The New Strong's exhaustive concordance of the Bible*. Nashville, TN: Thomas Nelson Publishers, 2010.

Chapter 1

Balaam's Parable of Aloe Trees
Numbers 24:1–9

The parable of the aloe and cedar trees was an oracle spoken by Balaam in Moab. Often the word *oracle* referred to a person, such as the oracle at Delphi; however, in this parable, oracle meant an authoritative decision or opinion. The third oracle given by Balaam named two trees—the aloe and cedar.

When the Moabites saw Moses and the children of Israel approaching their country, they were afraid the "horde" was going to destroy the land, i.e., cut trees for firewood, consume pasture lands needed for their own livestock. The Moabites wanted to turn the Israelites away. The problem was that Moab didn't have a standing army to fight against the Israelites. Until recently Moab was subjects of the Amorites. Moab was only freed from Amorite control when the Israelites successfully defeated Sihon, the Amorite king.

The canny King Balak didn't have the military might to stop the Israelites from crossing Moab. He decided to use guile to change the outcome of the conflict.

1. Change means: _____
_____

(Use a dictionary or your computer search engine to get a complete definition of change.)

To stop the Israelites, the Moabite king, Balak, sent for the most renowned seer/diviner in the known world—Balaam. King Balak planned for Balaam to curse the Israelites. In ancient times, people believed that cursing a person or people could influence their outcome. Balaam lived about four hundred miles north of Moab near the Euphrates River. When Moab envoys first approached him, Balaam refused to accompany them to Moab because God told Balaam not to curse the Israelites. Then, the Moabites sent a more distinguished delegation to Balaam and offered him even more money. God allowed Balaam to go with the Moabites; however, God warned Balaam that he could only speak the words God gave him.

Every Sunday school child knows what happened next: Balaam was riding a donkey toward Moab when suddenly the normally reliable donkey stopped in the middle of the path. The donkey refused to move forward despite Balaam hitting it with a stick. When the donkey started to talk, Balaam's eyes were opened. He saw an angel blocking the donkey's pathway. Alarmed, Balaam offered to return to his home in Pethor. The angel directed Balaam to go to Moab; but to speak only the words God gave to him.

In Moab, Balaam gave five separate oracles or parables directed at the Israelites. Much to King Balak's disappointment, the parables didn't curse the Israelites. In fact, Balaam's oracles blessed the Israelites! In his third parable, Balaam compared the Israelites to aloe and cedar trees planted by God in watered land:

> How beautiful are your tents, O Jacob, your dwelling places, O Israel! Like valleys they spread out, like gardens beside a river, like aloes planted by the LORD, like cedars beside the waters. Water will flow from their buckets; their seed will have abundant water. Their king will be greater than Agag; their kingdom will be exalted. (Numbers 24:5–7, NIV)

Aloe Tree

AGARWOOD

Maria Lin

cedar appears in several parables, it will be
tail later. In this parable, the aloe is emphasized.
the aloe of the New Testament which came from
plant, Old Testament aloe came from a tree. In
the ancient Near East, Old Testament aloe was from the eaglewood tree. Likely, Old Testament traders brought aloe wood
from India. The Indian eaglewood is a massive evergreen that
grows to 131 feet tall with a trunk (bole) of four to eight feet in
diameter. Ancient Middle East people believed that the aloe tree
was descended from a tree in the Garden of Eden. According to
legend, Adam brought aloe tree shoots from Eden and planted
them where he and Eve settled.

Aloe is made from agarwood in the eaglewood tree, but only
about 10 percent of mature eaglewood trees produce agarwood.
The fragrant oleoresin that permeates the heartwood of some
eaglewood trees is produced by a fungal infection. Once the
fungus establishes itself on the tree, the woody trunk turns a
deep brown color. The darker the agarwood, the more valuable
the aloe. Trees over fifty years old produce the best agarwood.
Agarwood is harvested, cut into small pieces, and burned. The
result is a distinct aroma described as being a cross between san-
dalwood and balsam.

**Agarwood gives off a pleasant fragrance or aroma.
Several places in the Bible we learn that the sacrifices
of the Israelites were a sweet aroma to God.**

1. Read and summarize (don't just write them out) each
verse about what is a pleasing aroma to God:

    a) Genesis 8:21

    b) Exodus 29:18

    c) Leviticus 3:16

2. How did sacrifices change from the Old Testament to post–Jesus New Testament times?

Because the eaglewood tree grew in India, likely Balaam never saw one growing in nature. When he included aloe trees in the parable, possibly Balaam referred to the sweet smell of aloe. His point was that the aroma of the Israelites was attractive. Yet, this interpretation doesn't reflect Balaam's words about growth of the eaglewood tree. More probably, Balaam heard traders' descriptions of the majesty of aloe-producing trees. Something in or about the Israelite encampment resonated with descriptions Balaam heard of the uprightness of aloe trees.

The Bible story of King Balak recruiting Balaam to curse the Israelites occurred as the Israelites were making their final push into the Promised Land. If Balaam viewed the Israelite encampment immediately after the Israelites left Egypt, he wouldn't have compared them to upright aloe trees. As former slaves, their backs were bent, their heads bowed. In contrast, the current Israelites came to adulthood as free men and women. They stood upright. They lived in the dry, rugged Sinai. They were used to standing tall to look into the distance for the first sign of danger to their families or for signs of water and food.

Balaam was smart and knew his craft well. He knew the Israelite history. He knew how they left Egypt. He knew about their forty-year trek in the wilderness. Possibly, Balaam compared the fifty years it took the eaglewood tree to produce mature agarwood (aloes) with the forty years the Israelites wandered in the desert while they coalesced into a nation. Alternatively, Balaam could have been thinking that only a small number of aloe trees convert to agarwood and sweet smelling aloes. So too the children of Israel were a small number, or percentage, of the world's population. Yet this small nation was unique in being God's chosen people; they were a sweet aroma to God. Finally, Balaam may have known that aloe trees grew in a variety of environments. Eaglewood trees adapted to different habitats, e.g., rock, limestone, sand, well-drained slopes and ridges, and land near swamps. Similarly, Jacob's offspring lived in and adapted to a variety of living environments, i.e., Canaan, in the Nile River delta, in the Sinai Desert, and now in Moab.

How are you, or could you be, a sweet aroma to God? List at least three actions—changes in your life—that would make you more fragrant to God.

a. _____

b. _____

c. _____

The spiritual interpretation of Balaam's parable is: what God has declared blessed, man shouldn't curse. The opposite is also true, what God has declared as sinful, damaged, and depraved, man can't declare as valuable and good. Perhaps an application is that we are to grow and fulfill our potential in whatever environment God sets us; like agarwood (aloe), we should be a sweet aroma to God, where he put us.

Think about your national culture and society. Have you seen any events and happenings declared okay or permissible in society that God declared sinful, damaging, or depraved? Identify three examples:

a. _____

b. _____

c. _____

As a Christian in today's society, what is your role in restoring society to God's standards?

If we leave the story of Balaam at this point, we could conclude that Balaam wasn't such a bad guy. After all, he followed God's direction and didn't curse the Israelites. But there is more to the story of Balaam. The Bible recorded that after giving a fifth oracle, Balaam returned home. We assume he went back to Pethor, but Balaam didn't stay there. The Israelites killed Balaam along with the five Midian kings in a battle east-northeast of the Dead Sea (Numbers 31). The Israelites were justified in killing Balaam. He was responsible for advising the Moabites and Midianites to use women to seduce Israelite men to sexual immorality and idol worship. This advice led to the slaughter of over twenty-four thousand Israelites.

> **Only 10 percent of the eaglewood tree becomes sweet-smelling aloes and then only after it is infected by a fungus. How could you be a more sweet-smelling aroma for Christ? What changes would you need to make in your life?**

Chapter 2

Trees Crown a King

Judges 9

Technically, the parable of the trees is a fable because plants don't speak. In the ancient Near East, people were familiar with fables. Hearers knew the fictitious story had a moral that applied to everyday life. Often they discussed, even argued, the story to figure out its interpretation and application.

Actions of the Israelite judge, Gideon, are important to this parable. Called by God, Gideon was from the tribe of Manasseh; his home was in the Jezreel Valley. Gideon led the Israelites to throw off the seven-year tyranny of the maundering Midianites. One of the many positive characteristics of Gideon was his refusal to be king over the Israelites after he defeated the Midianites. His words were, "I will not rule over you, nor will my son rule over you. The Lord will rule over you" (Judges 8:23, NIV). Gideon had seventy sons by his wives and one son, Abimelech, by his concubine. Abimelech lived with his mother's people in Shechem. Abimelech's name means "my father is king."

After Gideon's death (1122 BC), Abimelech negotiated with his uncles and men of Shechem to crown him king. Abimelech and a group of paid adventurers murdered Gideon's legitimate sons with the exception of the youngest, Jotham. Abimelech's coronation occurred at the great oak tree at Shechem. At this site Joshua had made a covenant between God and the Israelites. He recorded God's decrees and laws in the Book of the Law of God (Joshua 24:25–26). In the approximately 250 years between Joshua (c. 1375 BC) and Gideon's deaths, these Israelites moved from belief that God was their king to putting their confidence in an earthly king.

When the Israelites entered the Promised Land, God instructed them to kill all of the Canaanites. They ignored God's command and allowed many Canaanites to live.

1. How could the situation with Jotham, Abimelech, and the Shechemites have been avoided?

2. Identify times when you ignored God's instructions. How did those times work out for you?

3. Identify what you would or could do differently. Don't you wish hindsight was foresight?

When Jotham gave this parable, he was heart sick. Not only had his father, the stable person in his life, died, but his half-brother murdered every other brother. Although the Bible doesn't say so, likely Abimelech seized all of Gideon and his brothers' lands. Jotham, legitimate son of Gideon, was left with nothing. On top of everything else, the men of Shechem and surrounding areas proclaimed Abimelech king! Jotham was outraged by the injustice perpetrated by Abimelech and the same people Gideon fought to free from the rapacious Midianites.

On the day that Abimelech was crowned, Jotham climbed to the top of Mount Gerizim and loudly proclaimed this parable:

> Listen to me, citizens of Shechem, so that God may listen to you. One day the trees went out to anoint a king for themselves. They said to the olive tree, Be our king. But the olive tree answered, Should I give up my oil, by which both gods and humans are honored, to hold sway over the trees? Next, the trees said to the fig tree, Come and be our king. But the fig tree replied, Should I give up my fruit, so good and sweet, to hold sway over the trees? Then the trees said to the vine, Come and be our king. But the vine answered, Should I give up my wine, which cheers both gods and humans, to hold sway over the trees? Finally all

the trees said to the thornbush, Come and be our king. The
thornbush said to the trees, If you really want to anoint me
king over you, come and take refuge in my shade; but if
not, then let fire come out of the thornbush and consume
the cedars of Lebanon! (Judges 9:7–15, NIV)

Jotham didn't stop with a parable, he included a curse. Jotham's
curse was that if the people acted honorably toward Gideon who
fought for them and rescued them from the Midianites, then
Jotham wished them joy in their new king. However, if they acted
dishonorably, then let fire come out of Abimelech and consume
the citizens of Shechem and Beth Millo and let fire come out of
the two towns and consume Abimelech. After giving the parable and curse, Jotham fled south to Beersheba. Jotham made his
home at Beersheba because he feared Abimelech.

**Have you ever wondered how Jotham's life turned out?
How do you feel about what God allowed to happen to him?**

1. How does Romans 6:23 apply to Jotham's life?

2. Do you believe that Jotham ignored any of God's instruc-
    tions? Explain your answer.

3. What is your answer to the age-old question of why bad
    things happen to good people?

Before the Israelites entered the Promised Land, God told
them that the land would be filled with wheat, barley, vines, fig
trees, pomegranate trees, olive oil, and honey. These seven species
contributed to the quality of life of the Israelites. According to
Jotham's parable, when the trees decided they wanted a king, the
first tree they asked was an olive tree, then a fig tree, and then the
grape vine. Olives, figs, and grapes were eaten fresh, dried and
eaten over the winter months, or made into other products that
enriched the Israelite's food supply. All three plants refused to
accept kingship over the trees. Each had the same rationale: what

they contributed to mankind's welfare was better than taking the responsibilities of kingship. The three plants represented Gideon, his sons, and other Israelite leaders.

After exhausting other avenues to secure a king, the trees approached the thornbush and asked it to become king. The thornbush agreed with the caveat that the trees rest in its shade. Resting in a king's shade was a common euphemism for a king caring for the people he ruled and for the people submitting to the king's will. The thornbush said if the other trees refused to rest in its shade, then its fire would consume the cedars of Lebanon. Essentially, the thornbush threatened that if it was crowned king, and then subjects refused to support it, the thornbush would destroy them. In Jotham's parable, Abimelech was the thornbush who agreed to be king after all honorable men declined. The cedars of Lebanon symbolized the Israelite people over whom Abimelech ruled.

Jotham's choice to use the thornbush as a symbol of Abimelech's lack of qualifications to be king demonstrated that he knew how thornbushes grew. The thornbush was known commonly as the *atad*.[1] It is larger than all, or many, fruit trees native to Israel. In the wild, the thornbush may grow thirty to thirty-five feet tall; consequently, at times it grows as a tree. Branches are dense and intertwined and sometimes drop downward, almost touching the ground.[1] When this happens, sunlight can't reach the area beneath the bush and little grows there. Each leaf has a pair of thorns. One hard thorn is straight, while the other is hooked. The thorns depicted how harshly King Abimelech would treat his subjects. Further, neither local citizens nor traders or travelers could rest safely beneath the thorn tree because of the dangers of low hanging branches and thorns.

Thorn tree   Maria Lin

The thornbush root system is deep and wide spreading. Frequently, thornbush roots leach all nourishment from the surrounding soil.[1,2] For fruit trees such as olive, fig, and pomegranate to grow successfully, farmers must first remove all thornbushes before planting fruit trees. Although Abimelech was king, his subjects wouldn't be able to grow under his kingship. Abimelech would leach resources from his subjects in much the same way that the thornbush leached nutrients from the soil. Jotham knew that other trees and smaller plants couldn't grow under thornbushes.

In Israel, this thornbush produces flowers between March and October. The fruit is yellow and small, less than one inch in diameter. Each fruit contains a large stone (pit) surrounded by fleshy pulp. Fruit is best eaten green and tastes like sour apples. In no way does the thornbush's fruit compare favorably to the olive, fig, or grape. In ancient Israel, thornbush fruit was only eaten by people who were very poor or in time of famine.

The overall worldly or physical interpretation of this fable/parable was that a) Abimelech was a lesser man than Gideon, b) Abimelech's reign would be disastrous for the Israelites whom he ruled, and c) fruit of Abimelech's reign would be less than the present situation where the Israelites were ruled by God and his appointed judges.

The spiritual interpretation of Jotham's parable and this horrific situation is that when we move ahead of God's timing, the outcome is suboptimal, if not disastrous. God's choice for the first human king of the Israelites, King Saul, wasn't crowned for another seventy plus years. At this time (immediately post Gideon) in Israelite history, God's plan was for the Israelites to have judges as leaders. When the Israelites went their own way and crowned a king, the result was inferior to God's plan for them.

Why do you think that Abimelech wanted to be king?

1. Did Abimelech's love of power separate him from God or was some other sin occurring in his life? If another sin, what do you think it was?

2. God had a plan for Abimelech's life which Abimelech negated by his actions. What are some alternate ways that Abimelech could have acted, along with possible outcomes?

3. How does Romans 6:23 apply to Abimelech's life?

The Bible recorded what happened under Abimelech's kingship. After three years, God sent an evil spirit between Abimelech and the Shechemites. We aren't sure how the evil spirit worked. Perhaps, after becoming king, Abimelech had time to think about his status. True, he was undisputed king because he killed all opposition; however, his backers were mercenaries. They only acted when they were paid. Further, the townsmen who supported Abimelech were the type of men who condoned the murder of Gideon's sons. How secure was his throne? How likely was it that his sons would succeed him as king? Townsmen over whom King Abimelech ruled may have had second thoughts also. They remembered Gideon's words that God should rule over them, not a man. They couldn't trust a man who slaughtered his seventy brothers. Some Shechemites ambushed and robbed people who passed by Shechem, thus thumbing their nose at Abimelech and his "power" to keep the peace.

The Bible recorded that a man named Gaal and his brothers moved into Shechem. Gaal was a Canaanite. Many men turned from King Abimelech and started to follow Gaal. While Gaal and his followers were eating and drinking, they cursed Abimelech. Abimelech heard about their disrespect and attacked Gaal and Shechem. Gaal was ousted from Shechem; however, Abimelech wasn't satisfied. He attacked and captured Shechem. About one thousand men and women took refuge in the tower. Abimelech ordered his men to gather branches from Mount Zalmon. These branches he piled against the tower and set them on fire. All one thousand people in the tower died from the fire, heat, and smoke. The Bible didn't identify the types of trees or branches used to burn the Shechem tower, but likely the thornbush was included among them.

Not satisfied with destroying Shechem, King Abimelech and his army went to Thebez and captured the town. He attacked Thebez's tower. A woman inside the tower dropped a millstone that cracked Abimelech's skull. Abimelech didn't want it known that a woman killed him so he persuaded his servant to kill him. When Abimelech's followers saw that he was dead, they went home; thus ended the short three- to five-year reign of the first king of Israel. Jotham's curse came true. Fire came out of the thornbush (Abimelech) and destroyed the citizens who supported him. Out of the towns Abimelech ruled came fire—in this case rebellion—that caused King Abimelech's death.

Do you think that Jotham's parable and curse had any impact on the outcome of this Bible story? If so, how did the parable/curse influence or impact the outcome?

References

1. Hareuveni, Nogah, and Helen Frenkley. *Tree and shrub in our biblical heritage*. Kiryat Ono, Israel: Neot Kedumim Limited, 1989.

2. Modzelevich, Martha. *Flowers in Israel*. http://www.flowers-inisrael.com, 2016.

Chapter 3

The Thistle and the Cedar
2 Chronicles 25:17–18

The parable of the cedar and the thistle is technically a fable. In it one plant speaks to another, i.e., the thistle to the cedar of Lebanon. Some Bible commentators called this parable a riddle because certain words King Jehoash spoke were difficult to interpret. When King Jehoash of Israel delivered the parable to King Amaziah of Judah, he also gave a warning to Judah's king.

The context includes previous events in both the Northern Kingdom (Israel) and the Southern Kingdom (Judah). Jehoash was king of Israel, which included ten Israelite tribes. Although an idol worshipper, King Jehoash visited the prophet Elisha and wept over Elisha's ill health. Because God had compassion on Israel, he allowed King Jehoash to defeat the Aram army in battle three times. Israelite towns, captured by the Arameans, were returned to Israel. King Jehoash was very capable as a military leader.

In Judah (composed of the tribes of Judah and Benjamin), Amaziah was king. Initially, King Amaziah followed God. He determined to finish subjugating Edom, started by his father King Joash. King Amaziah mustered an army of three hundred thousand fighting men from Judah and Benjamin. In addition, he hired one hundred thousand soldiers from Israel, paying them upfront a hundred talents of silver.

Then, a man of God came to King Amaziah. The prophet told King Amaziah that if he took Northern Kingdom soldiers with him into battle, God would cause him to lose the battle with Edom. King Amaziah believed the man of God. He sent the Israelite soldiers home, letting them keep the money he paid them. The Israelite soldiers were furious. They wanted the opportunity to fight in the battle and to plunder rich Edomite lands. Plunder, not payment for fighting, was the major source of riches for soldiers in the ancient Near East. While King Amaziah was fighting the Edomites, these same Northern Kingdom soldiers raided towns that belonged to Judah. They killed three thousand people and carried off great quantities of plunder.

King Amaziah led his army to the Valley of Salt where they killed ten thousand Edomites outright. They captured another ten thousand Edomite soldiers who they killed. When King Amaziah returned from battling the Edomites, he brought back idols of the gods of Seir, Edom's chief city. King Amaziah set the idols up in Jerusalem, bowed down to them, and burned sacrifices to the idols.

Why did King Amaziah bring the Seir gods/idols back to Jerusalem and worship them?

1. Read Exodus 20:1–6. What does God say about idol worship?

2. How were Israelites to deal with idols they captured or came upon in wars with other nations? See Deuteronomy 12:1–3.

3. Why do you think that King Amaziah failed to follow God's instructions?

God was angry with King Amaziah for his idol worship and sent a prophet to him. The prophet asked the king, "Why do you consult this people's gods, which could not save their own people from your hand?" (2 Chronicles 25:15, NIV). While the prophet was speaking, King Amaziah interrupted him and told the prophet that if he continued to speak he would be killed. The prophet stopped, but told King Amaziah that God would destroy the king because he worshipped idols and wouldn't listen to the prophet's counsel.

Why consult a god of a conquered people?

1. Do you think the man of God who warned King Amaziah not to take Israel's soldiers into battle against the Edomites was the same prophet who reprimanded King Amaziah against worshiping idols? Explain your thoughts.

2. Why did King Amaziah implement the man of God's advice about not taking Israel's soldiers into battle, but decidedly reject the prophet's rebuke on idol worship?

After consulting with his advisors, King Amaziah sent a message to King Jehoash to meet him face-to-face. In other words, Amaziah challenged Jehoash to battle. Likely, the reason for Amaziah's challenge was Israel's plunder of Judah's lands while Amaziah was fighting the Edomites. Because a king's subjects paid taxes, they expected their king to keep them safe. As king of Judah, Amaziah couldn't ignore Israel's murder of three thousand individuals or their plunder of Judah's land.

Rather than immediately agreeing to Amaziah's challenge, Jehoash sent a message back to Amaziah in the form of a parable and a warning:

> A thistle in Lebanon sent a message to a cedar in Lebanon, "Give your daughter to my son in marriage." Then a wild beast in Lebanon came along and trampled the thistle underfoot. You say to yourself that you have defeated Edom, and now you are arrogant and proud. But stay at home! Why ask for trouble and cause your own downfall and that of Judah also? (2 Chronicles 25:18–19, NIV)

In the parable, King Jehoash of Israel referred to Israel and himself as a mighty cedar of Lebanon and King Amaziah and

Judah as a lowly thistle. By identifying himself and Israel as cedars of Lebanon, King Jehoash coopted for Israel the name "cedar of Lebanon," a term used to refer to the Israelite nation from before they entered the Promised Land. To King Jehoash, King Amaziah's challenge was as ludicrous as if he asked for Jehoash's daughter to wed his son. In ancient times, sons of kings married daughters of kings only if the kings were equals in terms of land and wealth. Clearly, King Jehoash perceived that there was no equality between himself and the King of Judah. He was the mighty cedar of Lebanon and much more powerful king than Amaziah.

King Jehoash referred to himself as a cedar of Lebanon and to King Amaziah as a common thistle. What an insult!

King Jehoash went further in his insult to King Amaziah by giving King Amaziah a warning: King Jehoash identified King Amaziah as arrogant because he defeated the Edomite, but King Amaziah was asking for trouble if he persisted with the challenge to Israel. A future battle would result in King Amaziah and Judah's downfall. King Jehoash was convinced that even though King Amaziah won a decisive victory over the Edomites, he and his army were more experienced. After all, they won three major battles against Aram, a noteworthy adversary. Further, Judah and Benjamin were composed of only two tribes versus the ten tribes of Israel. Israel had more fighting men than Judah.

In the Bible, about twenty different words are related to some type of prickly or thorny plant.[1] In Jehoash's parable, the Hebrew word for thistle is *choâch* or *hoah* and is associated with the *Scolymus* genus of plants. When King Jehoash named King Amaziah a thistle, possibly he was thinking of the spotted golden thistle.

Cedar of Lebanon   Golden thistle   Maria Lin

There is a huge difference in size and characteristics between a thistle and a cedar tree. In contrast to the spotted golden thistle which grows a maximum of three feet tall, the cedar can grow 120 feet and has a main trunk diameter of six to eight feet. The spotted golden thistle is an annual herbaceous plant that grows in abandoned fields and ditches and along paths and trails. Essentially, thistles are weeds. In contrast, cedars are evergreen trees that are beautiful in winter and summer. The cedar of Lebanon grows in mountainous and rocky soil, its roots extend deep into the ground. Cedars grow slowly; it takes centuries to produce a majestic cedar tree.

Spotted gold thistles have little if any value to man or animals. Leaves are oblong and prickly. For the most part, even livestock avoid the thistle. Yellow flowers bloom May to August, but have no noticeable scent. Cedar wood is durable, free from knots, and easy to work. The heart wood is warm red and beautifully grained. Cedars exude a gum or balsam which gives the tree an aromatic scent in which people take delight. Most insects dislike the smell and taste; consequently, they don't attack cedars. Cedar wood is resistant to fungal disease so doesn't readily develop dry and wet rot. An expert botanist, King Solomon knew the cedar tree's characteristics. For God's temple, Solomon used cedar trees from Lebanon rather than any tree in his own country, i.e., sycamore or box tree. Given the different characteristics and value of the two plants, who would want to be characterized as a thistle when the alternative was the cedar of Lebanon?

The spiritual interpretation of the parable King Jehoash offered to King Amaziah was that King Amaziah's pride would lead to his destruction. King Amaziah didn't comprehend that his success over Edom was due to God being on his side. After King Amaziah's decision to worship Edom idols and not allow God's prophet to advise him, God left King Amaziah. Now, he would go into battle against King Jehoash and Israel with no divine assistance.

Often, we may not act or even say things that indicate self pride, but we think about our accomplishment.

1. How did each king exhibit pride?

2. Can you remember a time in your life that your congratulated yourself on an accomplishment without giving God credit? How did that work out?

3. When you act proudly, how do you think individuals in your life feel about you?

The two kings met in battle at Beth Shemesh, a town in Judah near the border of Dan. The Bible gave no details about the battle, i.e., number of men on either side; however, in the battle King Jehoash captured King Amaziah. King Jehoash took King Amaziah to Jerusalem. There, King Jehoash tore down six hundred feet of Jerusalem's wall in an area that made Jerusalem most vulnerable to attack. Jehoash took gold and silver from God's temple along with the palace treasures. King Jehoash returned to Samaria with hostages from Judah. Some scholars believe King Jehoash took King Amaziah with him to Samaria. Only after King Jehoash died was King Amaziah returned to Judah.

King Amaziah lived about fifteen years after King Jehoash died. From the time Amaziah turned away from God, Jerusalem leaders conspired against him. At some point, King Amaziah fled Jerusalem to Lachish, fearing for his life. Nonetheless, Jerusalem conspirators sent men to Lachish and assassinated King Amaziah. King Amaziah's life and rule became as insignificant as a thistle which King Jehoash compared him to in the parable.

When pride comes, then comes disgrace, but with humility comes wisdom (Proverbs 11:2, NIV) How does wisdom come from humility?

Reference

1. Roth, Carolyn A. *Rooted in God*. Mustang, OK: Tate Publishing Enterprise. 2014.

Chapter 4

Transient Plants and Wicked Men
Psalm 37

Some Old Testament parables tell a complete story, e.g., trees crowning a king. Others are short. Sometimes they even appear terse. Whether long or short, each parable has a spiritual message that unfolds through ideas, incidents, or natural objects in the physical world. In Psalm 37, King David included three parables of one-to-two verses each. These short parables compared wicked, ruthless men to plants.

As we read Psalm 37, we imagine an older and wiser King David. He is no longer the brash aspirant to Israel's throne or a newly crowned king. This King David has seen a wide range of events and people in his lifetime. He acknowledged his sin of having Uriah killed so he could marry Bathsheba. He knew his daughter was raped, and subsequently dealt with the murder of Crown Prince Amnon. King David was deposed as Israel's king and fought a heartbreaking battle to regain his throne. God, who David adored, told David that his hands were too bloody to build God's temple.

King David wrote psalms before and after he became king of Israel. Many were written to praise God or they were prayers to God. In contrast, Psalm 37 is directed toward all who will listen.[1] David wrote this psalm to praise God and to teach individuals who heard it. In Psalm 37, some of the forty verses are discrete thoughts while others are two-verse couplets. All are loosely organized around the theme that wicked men perish while good men prosper. David averred that God views righteous (good) versus wicked individuals differently.

David had some friends and many loyal followers; but over his lifetime he experienced the plots of many enemies. In Psalm

37, he told righteous men, "Do not fret because of evil men or be envious of those who do wrong; for like the grass they will soon wither, like green plants they will soon die away" (Psalm 37:1–2, NIV). David was very clear about the outcome of wicked men: "But the wicked will perish: The Lord's enemies will be like the beauty of the fields, they will vanish" (Psalm 37:20, NIV). Because fields, flowers, and grass are reviewed with New Testament parables, I am going to focus on David's third plant parable in Psalm 37. David wrote:

> I have seen a wicked, ruthless man spreading himself like a green laurel tree. But he passed away, and behold, he was no more; though I sought him, he could not be found. (Psalm 37:35–36, ESV)

When you see wickedness and ruthlessness actions, you can identify them. Now take the time to define both of these words: wickedness and ruthlessness.

1. Identify a time or two that you acted wickedly or ruthlessly. What was happening at the time in your life?

2. Where was your trust in God at this time?

3. How can you be less wicked and less ruthless at home, work, church, or any setting you find yourself?

In this parable, King David compared a man to a tree that flourished. The man's activities, although wicked and ruthless, were successful. They spread beyond himself, his family, his community, and sometimes even his country. His actions were cruel and without pity. He didn't care how he achieved his wealth and influence. This is the man who took property from widows and orphans. But, and this "but" is reassuring, this merciless man disappeared. The parable doesn't tell the reader if he died or if his wickedness caught up with him. Perhaps someone even more wicked brought him down. David's parable tells readers only that the man "was no more." David even looked for the wicked man—perhaps David wanted to know if he was still wielded his power—but David couldn't find him.

Think, really think, about whether or not you trust God with events in your life.

1. Name one person, event, or thing you trusted God to handle *lately* in your life? How did that go? Did you take control back from God after giving it to him?

2. If you trust God with your life, how would you behave differently than you behave now?

3. Write down some very specific behaviors you would change.

    a. _____

    b. _____

    c. _____

Characteristics of the laurel tree make it a fitting comparison to the transience of wicked, ruthless men. In Israel, laurel trees are called the sweet bay laurel because bay leaves come from the tree. During David's reign, laurel trees grew wild from Mount Hermon in northern Israel southward through the Jezreel Valley and into the Judean mountains. Today most laurel trees are six to twelve feet tall; however, in ancient Israel, laurel trees grew to sixty feet. In Israel the laurel tree is evergreen, retaining green leaves year around. One way to identify it is to bruise or cut a leaf and smell the sweet aroma; the aroma is of a bay leaf. One of the most important attributes of laurel trees—and one that King David apparently knew—was that laurel trees thrive where they are planted. They tend to wilt and even die if they are moved repeatedly. Ideally, gardeners plant laurel trees and allow them to grow in place. Further, laurel trees are sensitive to cold and frost.

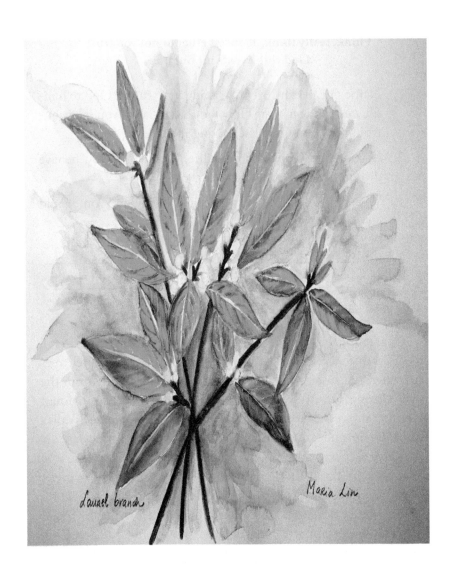

Laurel branch   Maria Lin

When King David wrote that he saw wicked and ruthless men who flourished like a green laurel tree in its native soil, he was thinking of a mature laurel tree with a broad canopy and numerous branches. This tree never suffered setbacks from transplanting. Likewise, prosperous, wicked men never seemed to have setbacks. Despite their seemingly charmed lives, David noted that later he looked for these wicked men. They were gone. David concluded that wicked men don't endure; they have no staying power. Perhaps, like a laurel tree, wicked men can't tolerate adversity—to include cold weather, frost, and transplanting. The laurel tree and a wicked man flourished but only in a narrow environment.

The spiritual focus of these parables is: righteous men and women's incentive to act right (using biblical moral-ethical standards) comes from knowing that ultimate power on earth and in heaven is in the hands of a just God. Even if righteous persons don't experience worldly prosperity, they are rewarded in heaven for how they acted on earth. In a later Psalm, David averred that the righteous flourish like a palm tree and like a cedar of Lebanon planted in the Lord's house (Psalm 92:12–14). Righteous men and women bear fruit in old age and stay both fresh and green.

In the three parables in Psalm 37, King David went beyond identifying the puzzle of seeing wicked individuals prosper. David advised not to fret when ruthless men (and women) prosper because fretting leads to evil. When David said evil, he meant anger, resentment, or mimicking wicked and ruthless men's business practices. Instead we should refrain from anger and hope in the Lord. Hoping in the Lord means we shoulder bad as well as good times from God. We accept cares and joy.

**Are there alternatives to anger and resentment at
seeing evil and ruthless individuals prosper?**

alm 37 and finish each sentence:

1. Verse 3: Trust _____

2. Verse 4: Delight _____

3. Verse 5: Commit _____

4. Verse 7: Be still _____

5. Verse 8: Refrain _____

6. Verse 27: Turn away _____

7. Verse 34: Wait for _____

8. Verse 37: Observe _____

In contrast to King David's parables that speak to the transience of wicked men, probably each us have seen wicked men and woman who have thrived their entire career, even life. Was David wrong in verses 35 to 36? What did he mean? MacDonald[2] wrote that King David may have been stating a general principle. He noted that Holy Scripture often makes sweeping statements; it describes a general, or normal, outcome of spiritual laws. Exceptions don't disprove the overall principles.

When we concentrate on flourishing in the garden where God planted us, we don't obsess about whether or not ruthless individuals are getting ahead.

References

1. Adeyemo, Tokunboh, ed. *Africa Bible commentary*. Grand Rapids, MI: Zondervan, 2006.

2. MacDonald, William. *Believer's Bible commentary*. Nashville, TN: Thomas Nelson Publishers, 1995.

Chapter 5

Parables of Vineyards
Psalm 80:8–13 and Isaiah 5:1–6

Do you want your heart to break? Then, read these two parables. Learn about the Israelites' rejection of God. Although written at two different times in Israelite history and by two different men, both parables are a cry of anguish from God to his chosen people. Both identify God as a gardener and Israelite as his vineyard. A vineyard and grapevines are synonyms with the nation of Israel (both Northern and Southern Kingdoms).

After the death of King Solomon, the Israelite kingdom divided (c. 930 BC). The Northern Kingdom, called Israel, included ten tribes: Ephraim, Manasseh, Dan, Zebulun, Asher, Naphtali, Issachar, Gad, Reuben, and Simeon. Some of the greatest Israelite prophets, Elijah and Elisha, lived in the Northern Kingdom. The Southern Kingdom was known as Judah. At times Judah included both the tribes of Judah and Benjamin. At other times, Benjamin seemed more aligned with the Northern Kingdom. Levite towns were located in both Israel and Judah, but for the most part the Levites were associated with Judah and the Jerusalem temple.

The first Northern Kingdom king introduced idol worship, which was embraced by much of the population. God sent prophets, Elijah, Elisha, Amos, Hosea, and others, to warn Israel that their idol worship and flaunt of God's laws would cause God to reject them. All calls for repentance were ignored. After two hundred years (c. 722–721 Bc), Assyria conquered the Northern Kingdom. Most of its inhabitants were exiled throughout the Assyrian Empire.

In the Southern Kingdom, Judah, descendants of King David ruled until 586 BC. Despite warnings and calls for repentance by prophets, i.e., Isaiah, Jeremiah, and Ezekiel, Judah turned from God to worship a myriad of idols. Jerusalem fell to the onslaught of the Babylonians. Most citizens not killed were taken captive to Babylon.

> **In their pride both the Northern and Southern Kingdom forgot that God was their hedge. They believed that their armies were protection for their borders and for their populations.**

List three things that your nation puts confidence in rather than in God.

a. _____

b. _____

c. _____

Bible scholars believe that Psalm 80, a lament, was written in response to the fall of the Northern Kingdom. The psalmist was from the family of Asaph, a Levite singer, poet, and head of King David's choir. Likely, Psalm 80 was written in Jerusalem from where the Northern Kingdom collapse was closely observed:

> You transplanted a vine from Egypt; you drove out the nations and planted it. You cleared the ground for it, and it took root and filled the land. The mountains were covered with its shade, the mighty cedars with its branches. Its branches reached as far as the Sea, its shoots as far as the River. Why have you broken down its walls so that all who pass by pick its grapes? Boars from the forest ravage it, and insects from the fields feed on it. (Psalm 80:8–13, NIV)

Isaiah's parable used a similar comparison of a gardener who planted a vineyard. Only instead of lamenting the downfall of the Northern Kingdom, Isaiah identified the fate of Judah. The song of the vineyard is a love song that described God's love and care for his people, how they rejected him, and ultimately God's punishment of Judah:

> I will sing for the one I love a song about his vineyard: My loved one had a vineyard on a fertile hillside. He dug it up and cleared it of stones and planted it with the choicest vines. He built a watchtower in it and cut out a winepress as well. Then he looked for a crop of good grapes, but it yielded only bad fruit. "Now you dwellers in Jerusalem and people of Judah, judge between me and my vineyard. What more could have been done for my vineyard than I have done for it? When I looked for good grapes, why did it yield only bad?
>
> Now I will tell you what I am going to do to my vineyard: I will take away its hedge, and it will be destroyed; I will break down its wall, and it will be trampled. I will make it a wasteland, neither pruned nor cultivated, and briers and thorns will grow there. I will command the clouds not to rain on it. (Isaiah 5:1–6, NIV)

On the physical or natural level, the parables of vineyards included preparing and protecting a vineyard. Parts of Canaan were ideally suited for vineyards and grape production. A single cluster of grapes could weigh twenty-four pounds. Remember the spies sent by Moses into Canaan (Number 13:23)? They returned with one cluster of grapes that required two men to carry. Grapes became a principal export of Israel under King Solomon. Hillsides, where wheat didn't grow well and cattle couldn't be pastured, were ideal sites for vineyards. In the Northern Kingdom, the hill country in Manasseh and Ephraim produced grapes and grape production occurred in Naphtali in the far north of Israel. In Judah, the area around Hebron, with its many hillsides, was perfect for vineyards. In En Gedi, vineyards were plentiful.

Usually, ancient Israelites enclosed vineyards with fences. Often farmers dug a ditch around the vineyard. The earth from the ditch was thrown to the inner side of the ditch. Then, fence posts and thorny plants were placed on the berm. At other times, a wall of stones or sun-dried mud took the place of the earthen fence with its thorny plants. Boulders and rocks were plentiful in Canaan. Large boulders were removed from the vineyard area and used for stone fences. Small stones weren't removed from the soil; their presence encouraged the soil to retain moisture, needed by the vineyard's soil.

Both the psalmist and Isaiah referenced vineyard fences. The psalmist asked God why he broke down the vineyard walls and removed its hedge so that all who passed could pick the grapes. Further, boars from the forest could ravage the vineyard. Isaiah prophesied that if Judah didn't repent, God would remove their walls and the country would be trampled. Briers and thorns would grow in the former vineyard.

For centuries Israelite vineyards had booths and watchmen who protected the vineyard from marauders. The booth became the watchman's home for the summer months. Sometimes a simple booth was constructed on a high spot where the watchman could view the entire vineyard. Frequently, it was made of tree branches and boughs, and provided shelter from the rays of the sun. At other times a more durable tower was constructed, especially if the watchman's family live with him during the summer months. These towers were from ten feet to an occasional forty feet tall. God set physical watchmen over his vineyard, Israel. The first watchmen were judges and then kings. Israel was to be a theocracy with God as their ultimate king. Israelites' first allegiance was to be to God.

Vineyard   Maria Lin

In Isaiah's parable, the vineyard was planted "with the choicest vine" (Isaiah 5:2). Farmers traded for the best vines available or purchased the highest quality vines that they could afford. As the vine grower devoted himself to the vineyard and grapes, God devoted himself to the children of Israel. He did everything possible to select good vines, protect them, and promote good growth in them. Yet, when God anticipated a yield of good grapes from his vineyard, he got only bad grapes. A Northern Kingdom prophet summed up what God wanted from his people: for them to act justly, love mercy, and walk humbly with him (Micah 6:8). God expected a yield of righteousness. Instead the people were disobedient, rebellious, and idolatrous. God was so disturbed that he asked: "What more could have been done for my vineyard than I have done for it?" (Isaiah 5:4, NIV).

> **We are judged by our actions. God looked for
> justice from the Israelites, but saw bloodshed.
> He looked for righteousness, but heard cries
> of distress from downtrodden people.**

1. Is doing nothing, i.e., keeping quiet when you see a wrong, a sin? How could silence be a sin? Isn't silence just self preservation?

2. Is God going to hold Christian's today accountable—will we reap the consequence—for doing nothing when we see a wrong?

The spiritual interpretation for both Psalm 80 and Isaiah 5:1–6 is that there are consequences of sin and both the Northern and Southern Kingdoms would experience those consequences. The consequence of Israel and Judah's sins was God abandoning them. God removed his protection from both kingdoms with the result that both were attacked and ruined and citizens were exiled. In their pride, both kingdoms forgot that God was their hedge. They believed that their armies were protection for their borders and for their populations.

In these two parables we can learn a second spiritual lesson: God's judgment is proportional. After becoming a nation separate from Judah, immediately Israel turned to idol worship, e.g., Jeroboam set a golden bull in Dan and Bethel and told Israel's citizens that the bulls were the gods that brought them out of Egypt. Over the next two hundred years, most of the nation's population repudiated God. In response, God allowed the nation of Israel to fall and most of its people to be exiled from the land. Although many of Judah's leaders and citizens rejected God through idol worship, some kings, i.e., Hezekiah and Josiah, initiated reforms and returned to worship of God. Although God removed his protection from Judah and Jerusalem and allowed the nation to be conquered by the Babylonians, God provided a way for these Jews to return to Jerusalem, rebuild the temple, and reestablish themselves as a nation.

Nations are made up of citizens, i.e., you and me.
Every Sunday in church, the pastor prays that
God will give us time for the amendment of our lives.

1. Read and even write out Psalm 51:4.

2. Name some thoughts and actions that are sins against God. I'll share one of mine to get you started. As a young woman I attended a "pro-choice rally." How could I have thought it was right to murder babies in the womb? God gave me time to repent and amend my life.

   a. _____

   b. _____

   c. _____

3. Is there anything in your life that you want to talk over with God and make amends for? Yes, I know that God knows all that we do, but God wants us to talk to him about these sins.

God gave the Israelites a bountiful land, good food, and protection. God expected that Israel and Judah would yield a crop of righteousness. Was God's expectation realistic? Did God expect too much?

Chapter 6

Crackling Thorns and Laughter of Fools
Ecclesiastes 7:6

The parable of crackling thorns is short, contained in one verse; yet, a comparison is made between the physical world and a spiritual truth. The parable attracts our attention, excites us, stimulates thought, and preserves truth. The crackling thorn parable was meant to be experienced by the ears. Indeed, we hear both crackling thorns as they burn and the loud boisterous laughter of fools.

The parable of cracking thorns was recorded in the book of Ecclesiastes. Ecclesiastes is part of the wisdom literature of the Hebrew people. Bible scholars aren't sure who wrote Ecclesiastes. Some suggested that Solomon authored the book. Others proposed that a citizen rather than a king was the writer and that Ecclesiastes was written long after the reign of Solomon. The writer referred to himself as "Teacher" (Ecclesiastes 1:1).

One idea in Ecclesiastes is that individuals should enjoy the life that God gives them. The author questions how mankind can live meaningfully, purposefully, and joyfully in the relatively short time allocated to each individual. Simultaneously, the Teacher answers his question by saying that a full life can be had if individuals place God at the center of all activities, i.e., work, family, church. The Teacher concluded that life under God was good, despite its multiple puzzles, paradoxes, and conundrums.

**What is there about a non-Christian life-style
that *looks* so appealing?**

1. Is it only to youth that this lifestyle appeals, or is it also attractive as we move forward in our careers, even in our marriages?

2. How can we stop ourselves from making bad decisions? Can we redeem the wasted years? Read Joel 2:25. What does God say about redeeming the wasted years?

3. Before wasted years can be redeemed, what do we need to do? Read Joel 1:12–14.

When Bible readers were asked what they learned from reading Ecclesiastes, many answered with some variation of "meaningless, meaningless, all of life is meaningless." With that answer, some proceeded to identify another Bible passage that told a more compelling story, stated a clearer principle for a Godly life, or prophesized an exciting end-time event. Yet, the Teacher's sometimes sly and thinly perceived wisdom gives direction for life to individuals who want to learn wisdom.

This parable that the Teacher wrote compared a fire of crackling thorns to the laughter of fools. In ancient Israel, cooking fires were in outer courtyards or inside homes. The time of year determined where the fire was located. In hot weather it was in the courtyard. In cooler or cold weather, the fire was located inside the home to add warmth. Many poor Israelites cooked over a simple hole in the ground (a fire pit) with rocks around it. Others had ovens, either inside the home or in the courtyard. Sources of fuel included wood, animal dung, and thornbushes.

The parable of crackling thorns is included in a chapter titled "The Contrast of Wisdom and Folly" (esv). Despite the chapter's name, the parable addressed folly, rather than wisdom. The parable reads:

> Like the crackling of thorns under the pot, so is the laughter of fools. This too is meaningless. (Ecclesiastes 7:6, niv)

When the Teacher concluded the parable with, "This too is meaningless," he linked the laughter of fools to burning thornbushes. A closer look at the word *meaningless* showed that it means "futile" or "has no purpose." Synonyms are "pointless and ineffective;" while the antonym is "useful."

If you wanted to act less foolish and more wisely, where would you start?

1. What makes a person foolish? How do they act?
2. What makes a person wise? How do they act?
3. Are individuals wise in every situation? Are individuals foolish in every situation?

The thorn plant in Ecclesiastes 7:6 is the thorny burnet also named the prickly burnet. The Hebrew word for crackling is *qôwl* (*qôl*), an unused root word meaning a "voice" or "sound."[1] In present-day Israel, thorny burnet can be found from northern Mount Hermon through Eilat, in the far southern desert. Like fools and their laughter, thorny burnet is widespread.

When individuals used thorny burnet plants as cooking fuel, three plant characteristics are important: First, although the burnet plant grows in dense clumps, it isn't a good source of cooking heat. Dry thornbushes burn readily and thorn heat flares up quickly, but the fire dies down just as quickly. Thornbushes provide no sustained heat to cook a meal or bake bread as does heat generated from wood. Similarly, the laughter of a fool occurs readily, but soon ends as reality sets in, the amusing event passes, or the joke is over.

Thorny burnet

Maria Lin

Second, in Israel, thorny burnet flowers bloom at the end of the rainy season, e.g., February to April or earlier. Mature female flowers are set in four to five joined petals. The top of the petals are covered tips of sepals (modified leaves set around the petals) which makes the female flower resemble a covered pot. These flower "pots" are numerous. In a fire, flower "pots" produce a small explosion. Nevertheless, these sounds have no value to the production of heat for cooking. Although a thorny burnet fire may snap, crackle, and pop, and be pleasing to ears, the sound adds nothing to the heat. Similarly, a foolish person rejects the Lord for earthly pleasure and laughter, both of which are ultimately meaningless.

Third, skin on fingers and arms can be pricked by plant thorns when the thorny burnet is added to a fire. Similarly, when foolish individuals laugh at us—even when the laughter is short-lived—the laughter pricks us. True, we can look back and reflect on whether or not their loud laughter was appropriate or valuable, but, in the moment, the laughter hurts. This use of thorny burnet in the parable demonstrates how ridicule and laughter can hurt us and influence how we live our lives.

Ridicule and laughter can hurt us as we live out our lives. But there is an alternative!

1. People who make fun of others act foolishly. What does the fool say about God (Psalm 14:1)?

2. Is God with you when you are the butt of foolish laughter? Where is God at that time (Psalm 14:5)?

3. If you wanted God to be with you—so you can ignore when others make fun of you—what can you do?

Ecclesiastes 7:6 is one of two Bible verses which identified the thorny burnet; however, since Adam and Eve, thorns and thornbushes have played a role in agriculture and in parables. In the

Bible, thorny plants were often associated with desolation and ruin, i.e., enjoyments such as alcohol and carousing with friends leads to foolish laughter; but it also leads to desolation and ruin. Sometimes life on earth seems long, as year after year goes by. Yet, these seemingly long years are short when compared to eternity. So too is the seeming happiness of foolish decisions. For a short time, they may bring happiness, but in the long run, which includes eternity, they provide little joy.

The thorny burnet is widespread in Israel as are other thorny bushes. Ponder why thorns are so common in the Bible and included in multiple parables and other Bible stories.

Reference

1. Strong, James. *The New Strong's exhaustive concordance of the Bible.* Nashville, TN: Thomas Nelson Publishers, 2010

Chapter 7

Poem of a Plowman
Isaiah 28:24–29

The parable of the plowman is a two-stanza poem. The first stanza focuses on plowing the ground for planting and the second on threshing a crop. The poem ends with praise to God who taught mankind how to plant and harvest. Finally, the parable's interpretation unfolds.

Because Hebrew language and Hebrew poetry differ from English, native English speakers can't appreciate the memory cues in this Hebrew poem. We don't remember it in the same way that we remember, even memorize, Burns, Longfellow, and Whitman's poems. The parable of the plowman is an agriculture parable that resonated with farmers. The writer, Isaiah, was an urban agriculturist. Although Isaiah lived most of his life in Jerusalem, the content of Isaiah's book demonstrates a sure knowledge of the ways crops were planted, cultivated, and harvested. Isaiah saw visions and prophesized during the reigns of Kings Uzziah, Jotham, Ahaz, and Hezekiah. From Jerusalem he saw the final days of the Northern Kingdom. He warned the Southern Kingdom (Judah) that her sins would bring captivity. At the same time, Isaiah assured hearers that a remnant of Jews would be restored to Jerusalem and Judah.

The immediate context for the parable of the plowman begins in Isaiah 28:9. The country's leaders mocked Isaiah, but, more importantly, they mocked God. The leaders asked: Who is God to try to teach us? Are we babies? Are we newly weaned children? No! They were adults and didn't need detailed instructions from God, i.e., "Do and do, do and do, rule on rule, rule on rule, a little here, a little there" (Isaiah 28:10, NIV). The rulers in Jerusalem

Dr. CAROLYN A. ROTH

boasted they entered a covenant with death and the grave, thus, when a foreign nation invaded them, they wouldn't be touched (Isaiah 28:14–15).

According to Isaiah, reality for both Israel and Judah will be different. Neither country is prepared militarily or spiritually for foreign invasion, an invasion that God will allow in judgment for their rejection of him and his laws. Foreign soldiers will engulf Israel and Judah. Instead of God's words through a prophet, citizens will hear a foreign language spoken on foreign lips. Protection from death and the grave will be annulled. The people will be beaten down by the invaders, taken captive, and exiled. Judah's power politics that included reaching out to Egypt for protection from northern invaders, won't work.

Isaiah implored the Israelites to hear him four times, i.e., listen, hear, pay attention, and hear what I say (Isaiah 28:23). Isaiah wasn't speaking to hear his own voice, nor was he speaking his own thoughts and words. Instead, Isaiah gave God's message, a message vital to Judah's health and security:

> Listen and hear my voice; pay attention and hear what I say. When a farmer plows for planting, does he plow continually? Does he keep on breaking up and working the soil? When he has leveled the surface, does he not sow caraway and scatter cumin? Does he not plant wheat in its place, barley in its plot, and spelt in its field? His God instructs him and teaches him the right way.
>
> Caraway is not threshed with a sledge, nor is the wheel of a cart rolled over cumin; caraway is beaten out with a rod, and cumin with a stick. Grain must be ground to make bread; so one does not go on threshing it forever. The wheels of a threshing cart may be rolled over it, but one does not use horses to grind grain. All this also comes from the Lord Almighty, whose plan is wonderful, whose wisdom is magnificent. (Isaiah 28:24–29, NIV)

**Do you believe—really believe—that God taught
farmers how to prepare soil and plant seeds?**

1. Do you believe, as cultural anthropologist's propose, that agricultural methods were the result of trial and error?

2. Does God still teach mankind activities for living in the world? For example, do you believe that God taught computer analysts how to write computer code?

3. At some point, did God stop teaching man how to do things? Because mankind has evolved this far, are we now on our own, separate from God teaching us?

The parable of the plowman identified three activities a farmer used: breaking up the soil, sowing seed, and threshing the crop. The order of these three actions comes from God; they can't be implemented in a different sequence and still achieve an optimal harvest. Further, each class of seed requires its own soil, sowing method, and threshing.

Breaking up the soil: A farmer plowed his land; but, at a point when the soil was soft and ready to receive the seed, the farmer stopped plowing. Too fine plowing and repeated plowing wastes the farmer's time and contributes to top soil erosion and loss. Overplowing influenced the Dust Bowl in the 1930s in central United States.

Sowing seed: A farmer knew the best sowing techniques to get an optimal crop. He sowed caraway, scattered cumin, and planted the hard grains—wheat, barley, and spelt. The knowledgeable farmer even knew that hard grain seeds needed to be sowed differently. He didn't mix seeds together. He planted grain seed in their own plots, aware that they matured at different rates and were harvested at different times.

Threshing crops: The farmer knew how to thresh his crops to obtain a maximum yield. He beat the caraway with a rod (flail); however, cumin was extracted with a stick. Wheat, barley, and spelt were threshed using sledges or threshing wheels rotated by a donkey or ox.

In the parable of the plowman, two herbs were named. Although New International Version Bibles translate the first herb as caraway, other Bibles (AMP, ESV, KJV) translate this herb as fitches, dill, or fennel. Because the second herb, cumin, was translated uniformly in different Bibles, it is used as the prototype herb. Barley, a grain, is contrasted with cumin because of barley's historic significance to the Israelite nation.

Although cumin is an herb, it has the distinction of being the second most popular spice in the world. Probably, cumin originated in the Nile Valley. Israelites may have taken cumin seeds with them when they left Egypt. According to Isaiah, ancient Israelites scattered cumin on the top of prepared soil in the spring. Cumin seeds need a lot of water, but not a soggy environment. Growing conditions for cumin seeds parallel how Israelites—particularly the Northern Kingdom—overindulged themselves. Just as some water is good for cumin seeds and seedlings, some wealth and leisure are good for a nation, but excess leads to sin.

Cumin plants benefit from a little crowding. Ideally, they are grown in groups or clumps. Plants support each other, keeping stems from bending over and touching the ground. Similar to a cumin plant needing the support of other plants to grow optimally, Northern and Southern Kingdoms, i.e., all twelve tribes of Israel, needed each other for optimal growth. When Israel and Judah separated they didn't have each other for support. Both nations became vulnerable to outside attack.

Cumin seeds are ready to harvest when pods turn brown and dry. When this happens, pods open and spill their seeds onto the ground. Often, pods don't dry all at once, but need to be harvested at various times through the harvest season. Like cumin seeds, the sins of the Northern and Southern Kingdom matured at different rates. The Northern Kingdom, Israel, was destroyed almost two hundred years before Babylon razed Jerusalem.

Cumin

Barley

Maria Lin

In contrast to the herb cumin, barley is a grain. For Israelites, barley was a major food staple for several reasons. First, barley was less expensive to purchase than wheat. Second, barley was drought-resistant and grew in both alkaline and saline soils; consequently, barley grew in the diverse habitats of the Promised Land. Third, under favorable conditions, barley ripened in as few as sixty to seventy days, a shorter maturation time than wheat. In Israel, winter barley was sown in November and December and harvested in April or early May. Israelites were so closely associated with barley that Midianites referred to them as "barley cakes" (Judges 7:13).

While the wealthy Israelites made bread from wheat, poorer families used barley almost exclusively. For the poor, wheat flour was a luxury. As both the Northern and Southern Kingdoms aged, the separation between the wealthy who ate wheat bread and the poor who made bread from barley grew. Kings and leaders, insulated by their wealth, had almost no understanding of the everyday lives of the poor in their nations.

By the time Isaiah prophesized, Israelites used two-hand wooden plows with an iron point on the end; the iron point turned over the ground. Plows were pulled by an ox or oxen and guided by the farmer. Barley seeds were dropped in rows or furrows and covered by harrowing (or smoothing) the soil over seeds. Once ripe, barley stalks were cut using a scythe then transported to the threshing floor in wagons or in large baskets. Wealthy farmers had their own threshing floors, but more often a threshing floor was shared by a village or town. The threshing floor was publicly owned and located outside of the town wall. When Isaiah prophesized, there were four methods of threshing: a stick, animals, a threshing sledge, and a wheel.[1] The most common and effective method to thresh barley was with the sledge. A sledge was a platform made from two wooden boards. The front was upturned so it would not jam against the floor when pulled by animals. On the sledge bottom, hard stones and later iron was embedded to break the barley kernel from the stalks.

In order to achieve security for their land, citizens had to recognize and abide by God's rules just as planting herbs and grains followed agrarian rules. Unfortunately, in Israel and Judah, both leaders and citizens rejected God and God's requirements for national and personal holiness. There was little, if any, justice in either Israel or Judah. The result was God's judgment on each nation and its people.

Ponder the relationship between national sins and personal, individual sins.

1. What did prophets mean when they condemned nations as sinful?

2. When some people in a nation sin, is every citizen in the country guilty?

3. Is a nation responsible for the sins of citizens? Is a citizen responsible for the sins of a nation?

The analogy for the farmer selecting varied methods to sow different types of seed, i.e., herbs versus grains, demonstrates that God's judgments aren't arbitrary. God doesn't stereotype his people. Carefully, he selects the judgment and discipline suited for a person's needs. God uses the lightest possible touch. He never allows his judgment to be greater than his people can bear. Israel's sins were so detestable that the nation was destroyed. In contrast, God punished Judah for sins but didn't punish them forever. The punishment had an endpoint. A glorious future awaited the redeemed nation. As a farmer doesn't plow a field forever, so Judah's punishment won't last forever.

God doesn't have set punishment for sin. God punishes each individual who sins according to his/her level of knowledge and abilities.

1. Would a truly good God ever punish the people he created? Why or why not?

2. What would be the advantages and disadvantage of God having a stereotype response to each individual sin?

3. Paul wrote, "God does not judge by external appearance" (Galatians 2:6, NIV). Is it possible that what looks like the same sin in two different women could be different circumstances and sin? Should these two individuals be judged differently by God?

Often Bible commentators compared Isaiah's parable of the plowman to Jesus's teachings in the New Testament. Several asserted that Jesus's parable of the wheat and tares echoed Isaiah's plowman parable. Others suggested that Jesus's teaching in Matthew 16:2–4, where the Pharisees and Sadducees couldn't interpret signs of the times, had its origins in Isaiah's plowman parable. It makes sense that Jesus based his teachings and parable on Old Testament writings because the Holy Spirit—the third entity of the Trinity—gave the parables to Old Testament prophets and writers.

Individuals reap what they sow. How can you take the time to learn about God and his statutes so you sow wisely?

Reference

1. Borowski, Oded. *Agriculture in iron age Israel.* Winona Lake, IN: Eisenbrauns, 2009.

Chapter 8

Vision of an Almond Branch
Jeremiah 1:11–12

Most Old Testament parables were heard; they stimulated the ear and appealed to the auditory sense. The almond branch parable was different. God gave it to Jeremiah in a vision. Just because the parable was visual doesn't make it was less important. As with most messages from God, Jeremiah's record began with "The word of the Lord."

Jeremiah was from the priestly family of Hilkiah. His home was Anathoth, a short three to four miles northeast of Jerusalem. Bible scholars believe God called Jeremiah to be a prophet when Jeremiah was as young as twelve to thirteen years of age. By this point in history (about 627 BC), Assyria had conquered the Northern Kingdom (Israel). Many Israelites living there were exiled throughout the Assyrian Empire. The military and political powers in the Near East were Egypt, southwest of Judah, and Babylon to the east.

Shortly after God called Jeremiah to be his prophet, God gave Jeremiah two inaugural visions. The first encompassed an almond branch. The vision is sometimes regarded as part of God's training of Jeremiah to be a prophet. God expected Jeremiah to see and interpret the vision. Jeremiah was to use his senses and mind in service to God. Jeremiah had to participate in the explanation of God's message.

King Josiah (640–609 BC) was on Judah's throne; he initiated religious reforms to return Judah to worship of the true God. Jeremiah was a strong supporter of Josiah's actions. Unfortunately, after King Josiah's death, subsequent kings (Jehoahaz, Jehoiakim,

Jehoiachin, and Zedekiah) abandoned Josiah's reforms. In 586 BC, Jerusalem was destroyed by the Babylonians; however, when God gave Jeremiah the almond branch parable, Jerusalem's destruction was forty to fifty years in the future.

In this parable, God showed Jeremiah an almond branch. The vision was followed by questions and answers between God and Jeremiah. Jeremiah recorded:

> The word of the LORD came to me: "What do you see, Jeremiah?"
> "I see the branch of an almond tree," I replied.
> The LORD said to me, "You have seen correctly, for I am watching to see that my word is fulfilled." (Jeremiah 1:11–12, NIV)

My first reaction to this parable was, "What in the world? How does an almond tree relate to God watching to see that his word is fulfilled in the world?" Subsequent investigation showed that the Hebrew word for almond tree was *shâqêd*.[1] *Shâqêd* translates: to be alert, awake, sleepless, and on the lookout. For many centuries, even a millennium, the almond tree and blooms were symbols of watchfulness and wakefulness to the children of Israel.

**About one thousand years before God gave
Jeremiah the vision of the almond branch,
Job called God "a watcher of men."**

1. Read Job 7:20. Why do you think Job named God a watcher?

2. List some ways we can insure (as much as possible) that God sees righteousness when he looks at our lives?

   a. _____

   b. _____

   c. _____

3. What responsibility do we have to watch and intervene in the spiritual lives of men and women who don't know Christ, particularly for our family members?

The almond tree is the first tree to bloom in the new year in Israel; it wakes up early. Generally, the almond tree starts to flower the middle of February; however, in the Negev Desert, almond tree buds and blossoms are seen as early as January. Similar to the blooming of an almond tree, God recruited Jeremiah to be his prophet early in Jeremiah's life. Israelites grew and harvested almonds from sweet almond trees. The almond tree grew about thirty feet high and was often used for shade for people and livestock. Almonds were pressed into almond oil and occasionally almonds were ground and made into flour. Similar to the multiple uses of an almond tree, God communicated with Jeremiah multiple ways over Jeremiah's approximately four decades as a prophet. Further, Jeremiah communicated God's message to the nation of Judah in multiple ways, i.e., speaking, writing, and actions.

In the days of Jeremiah, both a male and a female flowering almond tree were needed for propagation. The need for a male and female almond tree to get an almond crop reminds me that in the disastrous years before the fall of Jerusalem, both men and women worshiped idols and turned from serving God. Neither husbands nor wives attempted to draw their spouses from idol worship to worship the living God.

In comparison to some other trees in the Promised Land, the almond tree is relatively short-lived. Young almond trees begin to produce almond crops in their third or fourth year of growth. Often Israelites cut almond trees down after twenty-five years; however, some almond trees are productive much longer, just as Jeremiah continued to be a productive prophet for God into his old age. A component of God's judgment on Judah, i.e., the Babylonian exile, was that it was relatively short-lived (seventy years), similar to the productive life span of most almond trees.

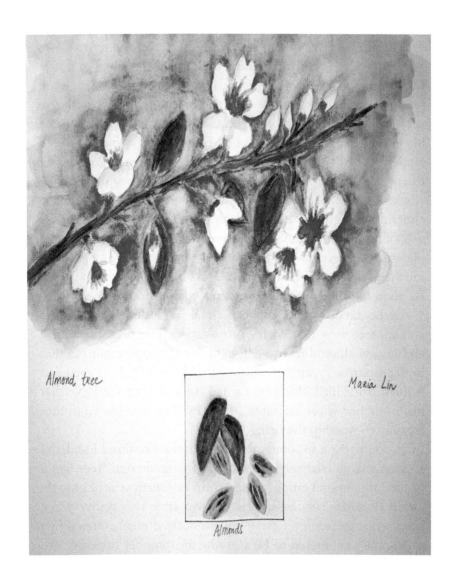

Almond tree

Maria Lin

Almonds

When God gave Jeremiah the parable of the almond branch, he gave Jeremiah its interpretation. The interpretation was that God was watching and alert to see that his word was fulfilled in Judah. When Jeremiah saw the almond branch with its blooming flowers, possibly he interpreted the vision as a message of hope for Judah. Unfortunately, subsequent visions God gave to Jeremiah carried little hope for Judah's immediate future. Just as the almond tree was a sign of spring, it symbolized and heralded the judgment that God pronounced on Judah through such prophets as Joel, Isaiah, and Zephaniah. The ruinous spiritual condition of Judah's people meant God had to destroy Judah before he could rebuild the nation.[2]

**As a child I visualized God watching
me like an "all seeing eye."
I was afraid God would see and
punish my offenses and sin.**

1. Do you think God is watching you, or do you perhaps say something like "God has more important things to do than pay attention to what I do."

2. Look up the following verses on God watching. Write a short description of what the verses say.

    a. Psalm 33:13–14

    b. Psalm 121:5

    c. Psalm 145:20

3. After reading these passages, would you conclude that God does, or doesn't, watch over you? Ponder that God watches us not to condemn, but to see ways to help us. God's action is the same: he watches; however, understanding of God's motivation for watching makes a huge difference in our anxiety level and walk with God.

DR. CAROLYN A. ROTH

In the Bible the almond tree was mentioned several places prior to Jeremiah's vision. When Jacob (approximately 1875 BC) directed his sons to go to Egypt to buy grain, he told them to take almonds as a gift to the Egyptian rulers. Several Bible historians contended that almonds were a delicacy only the very rich could afford; therefore, almonds were a valuable gift for an Egyptian pharaoh. Possibly, Joseph or the Israelites who settled Goshen introduced almond trees into Egypt.

The Israelites knew the beauty and significance of almond trees. Almond tree buds and blossoms appeared on the Tabernacle lamp stand (Exodus 25:33–34). Each of the six side branches and central branch was decorated with almond buds and flowers. Aaron's staff was made of almond wood. It was his staff that sprouted and produced almond buds, blossoms, and nuts when placed in front of the Ark of the Covenant overnight. In both instances—on the lamp stand and on Aaron's rod—the almond symbolized the need for the Israelites to watch that they obeyed God in all their actions. By the time of Jeremiah, the nation of Judah forgot God's warning to citizens, priests, and rulers to watch their beliefs and actions.

**Take out a one-dollar bill and look on the back side.
See the eye on the top of the pyramid.**

1. The two Latin phrases on the one-dollar bill are *Annuit Coeptis* which means "Providence Has Favored Our Undertakings" and *Novus Ordo Seclorum* which means "A New Order of the Ages." How can both refer to God as a watcher?

2. My ninety-nine-year-old friend keeps a one-dollar bill in her nursing home room. She says the eye reminds her that God is watching her and that the triangular sides of the pyramid remind her of the Trinity. I like her interpretation better than the historical meaning of the Great Seal

of the United States. What about you? Which meaning do you prefer?

In Ecclesiastes (12:5), almond tree blossoms are used politely to describe the white hair of aged men. Because Israelites valued old age, a comparison of an elderly man to a white almond tree blossom was a mark of respect. Male family elders were to be watchers so that Godly traditions and relationships were maintained in the family.

Do you remember the childhood rhyme: "Stop, look, and listen before you cross the street; use your eyes, use your ears, and then use your feet"? What would be the advantages of your learning to stop, look, and listen before you speak and use your eyes, use your ears, and then use your mouth?

References

1. Strong, James. *The New Strong's exhaustive concordance of the Bible.* Nashville, TN: Thomas Nelson Publishers, 2010.

2. Adeyemo, Tokunboh, ed. *Africa Bible commentary.* Grand Rapids, MI: Zondervan, 2006.

Chapter 9

Two Baskets of Figs

Jeremiah 24

Jeremiah's parable of two baskets of figs contrasted Judah captives taken to Babylon with those who remained in Jerusalem and Judah. The captives taken to Babylon were named "good," while those who remained in Judah were identified as "bad." Rarely in history are captives designated the "good guys," but, if we have learned anything about God, it is that he turns our preconceived ideas of right-wrong, rich-poor, and good-bad upside down.

By the time of this parable, Jeremiah had been God's prophet for about twenty-three years. In the years prior to Jeremiah's parable of the two baskets of figs, Judah's King Jehoiakim was murdered. His son, Jehoiachin, succeeded his father to the throne. After ruling three months and ten days, the eighteen-year-old king surrendered when Nebuchadnezzar besieged Jerusalem. This grandson of godly King Josiah, his mother and wives, capable fighting men, and the most skilled artisans and craftsmen were taken captive (597 BC) to Babylon. Nebuchadnezzar made Jehoiachin's uncle, Zedekiah, the vassal king in Judah.

In the parable of the two baskets of figs, God gave Jeremiah a vision that included a parable:

> After Jehoiachin son of Jehoiakim king of Judah and the officials, the skilled workers and the artisans of Judah were carried into exile from Jerusalem to Babylon by Nebuchadnezzar king of Babylon, the Lord showed me two baskets of figs placed in front of the temple of the Lord. One basket had very good figs, like those that ripen

early; the other basket had very bad figs, so bad they could not be eaten. (Jeremiah 24:1–3, NIV)

The reader isn't sure if Jeremiah was at the front of the Jerusalem temple when he saw the two baskets of figs, or if he was elsewhere and God included both the temple and baskets of figs in the vision. Immediately, Jeremiah noticed that one basket of figs contained good figs, which looked succulent and edible. In contrast, the second basket of figs was bad. The Bible didn't specify how the second basket of figs looked. Perhaps the figs were mushy, spoiled, or rotten, or they could have been small and dry. Whatever was wrong with these figs, they couldn't be eaten.

> Then the Lord asked me, "What do you see, Jeremiah?" "Figs," I answered. "The good ones are very good, but the bad ones are so bad they cannot be eaten." (Jeremiah 24:3–4, NIV)

The question that God asked Jeremiah in this parable is the same one he asked Jeremiah in the vision of the almond branch: "What do you see?" As with the first vision, God expected his prophet to not just look at, but to understand the vision. Jeremiah's response was accurate, he saw a basket of good figs and a basket of inedible, bad figs. Then, God interpreted the vision of two baskets of figs to Jeremiah:

> Then the word of the Lord came to me: This is what the Lord, the God of Israel, says: Like these good figs, I regard as good the exiles from Judah, whom I sent away from this place to the land of the Babylonians. My eyes will watch over them for their good, and I will bring them back to this land. I will build them up and not tear them down; I will plant them and not uproot them. I will give them a heart to know me, that I am the Lord. They will be my people, and I will be their God, for they will return to me with all their heart. (Jeremiah 24:4–7, NIV)

**God expected the captive Jews not
to resent their captivity or captors.**

1. Describe how you would feel if you were uprooted from your home and taken captive into another country.

2. How hard would it be for you to agree with God that you deserved exile as your punishment?

Jeremiah's use of the word *then* at the start of this section could imply a time lapse between God giving the vision to Jeremiah and giving its interpretation. Perhaps in the interim, God wanted Jeremiah to reflect on the vision, use his intelligence, and figure out the parable's meaning. Clearly, God regarded the exiles taken captive to Babylon as good figs. He planned to watch over them during their captivity and bring them back to Judah. God planned to build them up, not tear them down; and eventually God would replant the exiles in Judah. In addition, God would give the captives a heart to know him and they would turn to God with all their heart. The balance of Chapter 24 is God's interpretation of the basket of bad figs:

> But like the bad figs, which are so bad they cannot be eaten, says the Lord, so will I deal with Zedekiah king of Judah, his officials and the survivors from Jerusalem, whether they remain in this land or live in Egypt. I will make them abhorrent and an offense to all the kingdoms of the earth, a reproach and a byword, a curse and an object of ridicule, wherever I banish them. I will send the sword, famine and plague against them until they are destroyed from the land I gave to them and their ancestors. (Jeremiah 24:8–10, NIV)

In contrast to the good figs, the outcome for the bad figs was dire. The bad figs were King Zedekiah, his officials, and other survivors of the Babylonian siege of Jerusalem. God was going to send sword, famine, and plague on the people who remained in

Judah. Indeed, during the siege of Jerusalem, residents suffered famine and pestilence. When the Babylonians broke through the Jerusalem walls, soldiers murdered thousands of Jerusalemites. Survivors were exported to foreign kingdoms. God determined to make these exported Judahites abhorrent to the people of every kingdom where the Babylonians settled them.

**Captivity and exile were the price the Jews paid
for disobeying God by worshiping idols and
by treating fellow Israelites with contempt.**

1. Despite their bad behavior, many Judahites continued to make sacrifices at God's temple. Today we don't make burnt offerings to God. Instead we give money to the church and worthy charities. Is giving a tithe or offering sufficient to meet the requirement for a Godly life? Explain your answer.

2. What if most of our actions are Godly, but inside we are angry and resentful? Is exhibiting Godly behavior sufficient or do we have to have a change in our heart? How can we change our hearts?

3. Samuel told the Israelites that to obey God is better than to make sacrifices to him. How would you apply Samuel's words to your life?

Several characteristics of fig trees and their fruit make them a good illustration for Jeremiah's vision of the good and bad baskets of figs. Although a relatively small tree, fig trees figured prominently in Israelite lore and holy writings. Supposedly, Adam and Eve used fig leaves to first clothe their bodies. The fig leaves in the Adam and Eve account symbolized their disobedience to God in much the same way that most of Judah's people disobeyed God's laws. Although fig leaves are large (typically five to ten inches long and four to five inches wide) and even attractive, they are rough and hairy on the underside. When injured, leaves exude a bitter, sticky, and milky resin. Adam and Eve sewed several fig leaves together to create aprons to cover their naked bodies. These fig leaf clothes would have been itchy, sticky, and altogether uncomfortable against the skin. Judah's choices to disobey God and hide in their sin resulted in much more than mere discomfort.

Through Moses, God told the Israelites that the fig tree would be one of the seven species of plants that would enrich their lives in the Promised Land, yet fig trees aren't exceptionally hardy. They grow best in a narrow environment.[1] The average fig tree grows about twenty feet tall and develops a spreading canopy. The trunk is short; the bark gray and smooth. The tree trunk is sensitive to heat and sun and easily damaged. Further, fig trees can be damaged if temperatures drop to 30 degrees Fahrenheit. Perhaps, the bad figs in Jeremiah's parable came from a tree that received too much summer heat or were damaged by frost.

Sometimes figs grow under leaves and at other times above leaves. In the Middle East, fig trees can bear fruit twice a year.[2] The winter (first) fig crop ripens in June; the summer (second) crop ripens August through September. Often on fig trees, fruit (figs) appears prior to, or with, leaves. Remember, during Passover, Jesus walked to a fig tree on his way from Bethany to Jerusalem (Mark 11:12–14)? Because he saw leaves on the fig tree, Jesus expected the tree would contain figs he could eat. The fig tree contained leaves, but no figs. As with Jeremiah's basket of bad figs, Christ concluded the fig tree was useless. The proper response was to cut down the useless tree (Luke 13:6–9).

Unique among flowering trees, fig flowers aren't seen; rather, flowers are enclosed inside the fig (fruit) itself. Similar to the hidden fig flower, God wanted Judahites to produce good works, not for outward display, but to sweeten the lives of individuals around them. Unfortunately, the last four kings of Judah evidenced little, if any, good fruit in their lives. Individual citizens of Judah followed the lead of their kings.

Good Figs   Bad Figs

                                              Maria Lin

After four years of growth, most fig trees begin to produce fruit. Ideally, figs ripen fully before they are picked. A fig is ripe when it darkens, turns brown or purple, starts to bend at the neck, and is slightly soft to the touch. Because all figs don't ripen at the same time, harvest occurs over several months. To get the basket of bad figs, Judahites may have picked all of the figs at the same time; they didn't realize or care that some figs weren't ripe and wouldn't ripen off the tree branch.

Jeremiah's prophecy of the good and bad figs came true. When Jehoiachin arrived in Babylon, he was placed in prison. There he remained thirty-seven years. When Nebuchadnezzar died, his son Evil-Murdock became king over Babylon. King Evil-Murdock released Jehoiachin from prison, gave him an allowance, and a favored place at the king's high table for meals. Seventy years after Jehoiachin's captivity, his grandson, Zerubbabel, led the first fifty thousand Jews who left Babylon and returned to Jerusalem. God considered the exiled Jews as good figs.

> **I cried out, "Just tell me what you want me to learn from this situation so I can get past the mental pain."**

1. A number of years ago, I had a big professional disappointment and was mentally hurt. Why do we have to experience mental pain?

2. Physically, pain is a symptom that something is wrong in the body. If you had to ponder mental pain in your own life, can you see where it is a symptom? Explain your answer.

3. In retrospect, I am sure that God wanted me to experience the pain, so I would rely more on him and could empathize with other's pain and loss. Have you ever had such an experience? How did you react?

Meanwhile in Jerusalem, King Zedekiah rebelled against Babylon. Nebuchadnezzar returned to Jerusalem, laid siege to the city, killed King Zedekiah, and conquered Jerusalem and the surrounding towns. Nebuchadnezzar assigned Gedaliah, a politically moderate Jew, as governor of Judea. Governor Gedaliah established his capital at Mizpah. Ishmael, a member of Judah's former royal family, killed Gedaliah and the Babylonian soldiers with him. The remaining Jews knew that Nebuchadnezzar would be furious at Governor Gedaliah's murder. They fled to Egypt for safety. Not too many years later, Nebuchadnezzar invaded Egypt. During the invasion his army killed most of the Jews who fled there. Thus, the bad figs were destroyed.

> **Most Americans resonate to New Hampshire's state motto: "Live Free or Die." Yet, God told the Jewish captive to submit to their Babylonian captors. When they did so, they were "good figs." What was God's rationale for declaring the captives "good?"**

References

1. Dirr, Michael A. *Manual of woody landscape plants*. Champaign, IL: Stipes Publishing LLC, 2009.

2. Borowski, Oded. *Agriculture in iron age Israel*. Winona Lake, IN: Eisenbrauns, 2009.

Chapter 10

Parable of Famine Bread

Ezekiel 4

At times God instructed prophets to act out parables. About one-third of Ezekiel's parables were action parables. Some, but not all, were accompanied by words. In chapter 4, Ezekiel recorded how he acted out three parables—he uttered no words. Jews in Babylon had to interpret Ezekiel's actions. All three parables depicted the severity of the coming siege of Jerusalem.

Ezekiel was both a prophet and priest. He was taken to Babylon when King Nebuchadnezzar took Judah's King Jehoiachin and ten thousand captive from Jerusalem to Babylon (597 BC). At that time, Nebuchadnezzar established Zedekiah as puppet king over Judah. Although a captive, Ezekiel lived in his own house near the Chebar River. God called Ezekiel as a prophet after he was exiled to Babylon. Ezekiel was a stern man, very aware of his divine commission. Frequently, Ezekiel referred to the Jews as "a rebellious house."

In Jerusalem, King Zedekiah rebelled against Nebuchadnezzar after ruling five-to-six years. King Zedekiah ceased paying tribute to Babylon and asked Egypt for military assistance to throw off Babylonian rule. Subsequently, Nebuchadnezzar laid siege to Jerusalem. After about eighteen months, the Babylonian army breached the wall around Jerusalem.

When Nebuchadnezzar and his army started for Judah, Jerusalem was flooded with refugees fleeing the countryside. The influx was so great that private homes, inns, and the temple courtyard were crammed with people. The poor set up tents in the streets or laid down at night wherever they found an empty space. People and noise were everywhere; smoke billowed from cooking fires.

Although the situation was dire, it got worse after the Babylonians arrived and surrounded the city. No additional food supplies entered Jerusalem. Human and animal refuse couldn't be removed. Filth and stench were everywhere. Often dead bodies remained where individuals died, contributing to stench and disease. Many people inside Jerusalem starved to death or died from disease. Some mothers killed and ate their children for food.

How can malnutrition, starvation, and famine be nonphysical?

1. Define malnutrition, starvation, and famine. You may want to look up each word in a dictionary.

    a. Malnourished

    b. Starvation

    c. Famine

2. How does each word impact the others?

In Babylon, God instructed Ezekiel to act out the siege of Jerusalem. The first action parable used a clay tablet to depict the siege. The second had Ezekiel lying on his left side, followed by lying on his right side. The third parable encompassed plants. God told Ezekiel to use grains and legumes to prepare a loaf of bread.

> Take wheat and barley, beans and lentils, millet and spelt; put them in a storage jar and use them to make bread for yourself" Weigh out twenty shekels of food to eat each day and eat it at set times. Also measure out a sixth of a hin of water and drink it at set times. (Ezekiel 4:9–11, NIV)

Jewish dietary laws required Jews to make bread from only one type of flour, i.e., wheat, barley, millet, or spelt. Combining different flour sources in one vessel (container, bowl) was a desecration and contradicted Jewish dietary laws (Deuteronomy 22:9). Normally, legumes weren't used to make bread; however, extremely poor individuals used beans and occasionally lentils for bread flour. Mixing flour from several sources showed the scarcity of flour during the siege of Jerusalem.

Although bread from these flours was highly nutritious, the amount was below substance level. Ezekiel ate twenty shekels of bread daily or about eight to ten ounces (700 to 1,100 calories). Oil added more calories to the bread mix. A sixth of a hin of water is about one and a half pint or three eight-ounce cups. This amount of bread and water allowed Ezekiel to barely survive. God told Ezekiel that food and water would be so scarce in Jerusalem by the time the siege ended that people would be appalled when they saw the ravages of famine on each other (Ezekiel 4:17).

The next three verses were a conversation between God and Ezekiel about how the bread should be prepared (Ezekiel 4:12–15). Initially, God told Ezekiel to bake his bread over human dung. When Ezekiel objected, God allowed him to bake his bread over cow manure; however, during the Babylonian siege of Jerusalem, Jews didn't have the luxury of using animal dung for baking. Near the end of the siege, no animals were alive in the city. All had been slaughtered for food. No wood was left. Human excrement became the primary cooking fuel.

God ends Ezekiel's action parables by interpreting them. God said to Ezekiel:

> Son of man, I will cut off the supply of food in Jerusalem. The people will eat rationed food in anxiety and drink rationed water in despair. (Ezekiel 4:9–16, NIV)

The parables of the siege of Jerusalem were about coming judgment on Jerusalem. The people of Judah sinned so long and to such a degree that God removed his protection from around Jerusalem. When Ezekiel acted out the parables of the siege of Jerusalem, God still dwelled in the Jerusalem temple; however, before the Babylonians surrounded Jerusalem, God's presence left both the temple and Jerusalem (Ezekiel chapters 10 and 11). Importantly, Ezekiel's actions shouldn't be interpreted as sympathetic magic where something done to a model or person has a similar act in reality. True, Ezekiel making famine bread foreshadowed the starvation of the Jerusalemites, but God caused the famine, not Ezekiel's behavior or magic.

How was God's absence from the Temple and the Babylonian sacking of Jerusalem and destruction of the Temple related?

1. Do you think that famine would have come to Jerusalem or Jerusalem would have been sacked by the Babylonians if God's presence remained in the temple? As you ponder your answer, read and summarize what each of the three Bible references say:

    a. 2 Kings 16:1–5

    b. 2 Kings 19

    c. 2 Kings 22 and 23:1–27 (Be sure to read the last two verses, i.e., 2 Kings 23:26–27).

2. If you were starving and had only human excrement to cook your food over, would it make a difference to you as you ate the food? How did it impact the Jews in Jerusalem?

Broad bean   Maria Lin

The book of Ezekiel is one of the most detailed and well-known references to grains in the Bible, but we also learn, or relearn, that Israelites dried and ground legumes (bean and lentils) into bread flour. For a plant in this parable, I describe the bean. In ancient Israel, beans were planted in late fall and matured in the spring. Bean plants are hearty enough to live through mild frosts. Young bean pods are green, three-to-six inches long, and contain two to six seeds called beans. Pods lower on the stalk mature first, while pods nearer the top mature later. If harvesting is delayed until all pods are ripe, pods nearer the plant bottom split and beans are lost. I wonder if fewer Jews would have died, or been killed, if God initiated judgment on Jerusalem sooner than he did?

Despite our predisposition to consume meat, the multigrain and legume bread that God told Ezekiel to eat likely provided a complete protein meal. Meat protein is composed of amino acids, nine of which are essential. Grains and legumes contain amino acids, but none contain all the essential amino acids. However, what one type of grain or legume lacked, another contained. Made from grain and legumes, likely Ezekiel's bread contain the complete set of essential amino acids. If eaten in sufficient quantity, this multigrain and legume bread could have kept Ezekiel nourished. For the Jerusalemites, the challenge was having sufficient bread and calories to maintain life.

By combining bean and grain flour, God reminded Jerusalemites that they were more concerned about breaking relative minor dietary laws than with breaking the first commandment, i.e., "You shall have no other gods before me" (Exodus 20:3, NIV). In comparison to breaking the first commandment, combining grain and legume flour was a minor infraction. Equally, minor and relatively unimportant was the source of heat to bake the bread, i.e., use of human excrement rather than wood or animal dung.

The Babylonians laid siege to Jerusalem in 588–589 BC. About eighteen months later, the Jerusalem walls were breached. Nebuchadnezzar had no more patience with the rebellious Jews or his puppet king, Zedekiah. He had Zedekiah killed and the Jerusalem temple and major buildings destroyed. The wall around Jerusalem was razed. Many Jews not killed by famine and plague were killed by the Babylonian soldiers. Only the poorest Jews were allowed to remain in Judah.

Think about your life if the Holy Spirit left you.

1. Would you *feel* there was someone/something missing inside of you? Explain your feelings.

2. Do you think you would know *cognitively* (mentally) that someone/something is missing in your life? Explain how you would know.

3. How do you think your *behavior* (actions) would change or not change as a result of the absence of the Holy Spirit?

"The day is coming," declares the Sovereign Lord, "when I will send a famine through the land—not a famine of food or a thirst for water, but a famine of hearing the words of the Lord" (Amos 8:11, NIV).

What does that mean? What a promise! What is your response?

Chapter 11

God as an Evergreen Tree

Hosea 14:8

The parable of the green tree is one of the Bible's miniature parables. Not only is it brief, but it tends to be obscure. Obscure parables allow the Holy Spirit to call forth prayerful study, so parables are fully interpreted.[1] When Hosea spoke the parable of the evergreen tree, it stimulated the ears of the people who heard it. Today, we read the parable and visualize the majesty of a green tree.

Hosea was a prophet to the Northern Kingdom (Israel). Hosea lived and prophesized during the middle of eighth century BC, during the final tumultuous days of Israel when six kings reigned in twenty-five years. Most were murdered by their successors with only one effective transition from father to son. The major tribe of the Northern Kingdom of Israel was Ephraim. Frequently, Hosea referred to the Northern Kingdom as Ephraim.

Generally, we remember Hosea because God directed him to marry an adulterous woman. Many scholars consider Hosea and Gomer's story a parable in and of itself. Hosea's interactions with Gomer are contained in only the first three chapters of his book. In the other eleven chapters, Hosea implored the Northern Kingdom to repent so that God could heal their waywardness. Really?

**In the NIV Study Bible, the title of Hosea chapter 14 is:
"Repentance to Bring Blessing."**

1. Why does the Bible talk so much about repentance? What is repentance?

2. Surely, I don't need to repent, do I? After all my parents brought me up this way. Am I really responsible for my own behavior or are my parents responsible for my behavior?

3. If you are doing what everyone else is doing, how could you be doing anything wrong in God's eyes?

Hosea averred that Israel's disloyalty to God and idol worship was spiritual adultery. He identified Assyria as the source of God's judgment on the Northern tribes. Because Hosea came from the Northern Kingdom, he knew every pride and perversion of royalty and citizen alike. Yet, Hosea spoke of God's love, mercy, and forgiveness.

In the first three verses of Hosea chapter 14, Hosea exhorted Israel to do three things: a) stop sinning by worshiping idols their hands have made, b) ask God to forgive their sins, and c) return to worshiping God. Hosea assured Israel that Assyria can't save them, nor can war horses (from Egypt). God alone can save Israel.

The next four verses (Hosea 14:4–7) are a beautiful outline of how God will heal Israel's waywardness if only the nation will return to God. When we read the verses, our hearts rejoice at what God, even at this late time, is willing to do for Israel. God's healing is expressed using plant metaphors.

- God will be like the dew and Israel will blossom like a lily
- Like a cedar of Lebanon, Israel will send down roots and send up new growth
- Israel's splendor will be like an olive tree
- Israel's fragrance will be like a cedar and men will again live in its shelter

- Israel will flourish like grain and blossom like the grape vine
- Israel's fame will be like wine from Lebanon.

After assuring the Israelites that God can and will heal Israel, Hosea offered a parable. Initially, I read the parable in the New International Version (NIV) Study Bible; however, I disagreed with the NIV translation of the tree as a pine tree. The pine tree that grows in Israel is named the Aleppo (Syria) or Jerusalem pine. Although an evergreen, the Aleppo pine is short lived (seventy to a hundred years) and has a shallow root system. The pine tree is a poor example, and perhaps a poorer translation, of the tree in Hosea 14:8. Other Bible translations identified the tree as a cypress tree (AMP, RSV). Characteristics of the cypress make it a more likely candidate for a comparison with God. Here is the parable:

> O E'phraim, what have I to do with idols? It is I who answer and look after you. I am like an evergreen cypress, from me comes your fruit. (Hosea 14:8, RSV)

In verse 8, God told the Northern Kingdom he has nothing to do with idols. God is separate, different, and apart from idols and images people make with their hands. God wanted the northern tribes to forget about idols, to clear them from their minds. God is the one, the only one, who can answer prayer. God can look after the nation and people in it. Whether a golden calf at Bethel or an image under a tree, idols have nothing to do with the living God.

What idols do you worship in your life?
What do you put ahead of God?

1. How is your present worship of idols (prestige, popularity, career, money) better than worshiping God? How is your present worship of idols worse that worshiping God?

2. How can you stop serving and worshiping your idols and turn to God? Do you even want to do that or you are happy with the way you are?

3. If you admit your sin, repent, turn to God, and ask him to be king of your life, will you have to give up idols? Which ones?

    a. _____

    b. _____

    c. _____

In the Old Testament, God revealed in many places and ways that he wanted to protect his chosen people and make their lives better, e.g., lead them in green pastures and beside quiet waters (Psalm 23:1–2); heal, guide, restore, and comfort them (Isaiah 57:18); and give them the kingdom forever and ever (Daniel 7:18). Perhaps, nowhere is God's caring so forthrightly and succinctly presented as in Hosea 14:8. He told Israel that he, not an idol, answers them and looks after them. He is like a green cypress tree. From God comes Israel's fruit, both their food and their righteousness.

The wild cypress tree of Israel was commonly called the Mediterranean cypress. The cypress remains green year around. The cypress tree is large, strong, durable, and full of resin which acts as a barrier against water seeping into the wood. Cypress trees are enduring, typically living at least one thousand years. Ancient Middle Eastern peoples viewed the cypress as a symbol of immortality. In the Bible, the cypress wood ark carried eight individuals through the raging flood that destroyed life in the then-known world. The long-living cypress tree is a fit symbol of the ever-living God.

Ponder your life and your immortality.

1. How are life and immortality the same thing? How are life and immortality different?

2. Do you want an immortal life?

3. How could having immortal life be a good thing? How could it be a bad thing?

On the Mediterranean cypress, loosely hanging branches grow from the central column in a whorl. Branches are rounded and have small elongated needles for leaves. Cypress tree branches and stems grow close together. These growth patterns plus year-round needles means that people who take protection under a cypress tree have little exposure to rain or snow. Likewise, the thickness of branches means travelers who rest under the cypress are rarely exposed to the sun. What a wonderful analogy of how God wanted to protect Israel, from the sun, rain, and snow.

Instead of brightly blooming flowers, the cypress tree produces cones. The same tree produces both male and female cones. On the Mediterranean cypress, pollination of female cones occurs in the summer. After pollination, the female cone's green ovules turn to seed. Usually, fertile cones turn brown and drop to the ground the year following pollination. God promised that if Israel would follow him, the country would once again be fertile and green.

The parable's spiritual interpretation is that manmade idols aren't immortal; they aren't even alive. They are statues, man's creations. Some have ears but they can't hear. Some have mouths but they can't speak. Having a head is not the same as having a brain and mind. Immortality, including long life for an individual or a nation, comes only from God.

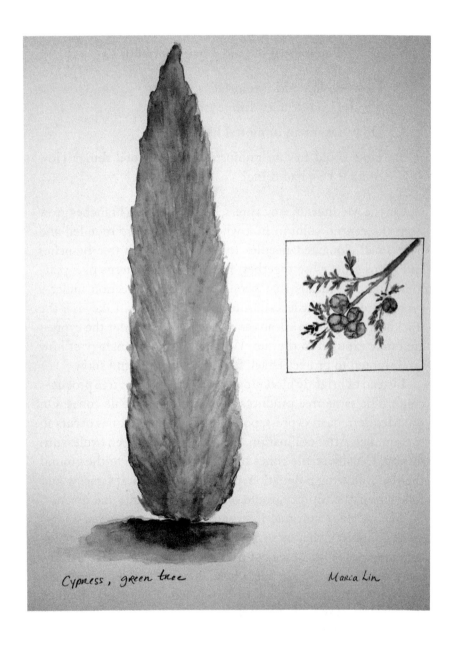

Cypress, green tree   Maria Lin

I read through the Bible several times; but, perhaps, unlike you, I never paid attention to Hosea 14:8. Hosea is a relatively murky book which other than the parts about Hosea and Gomer doesn't seem all that intriguing. But, this is the only place (that I know of) where God compared himself to a living organism. We know that God is enduring like the mountains, the soil, and the ocean. In Hosea, God likens himself to something alive, as he is alive. That living organism was a tree with a lovely smell and which was disease-resistant. Although ancient people used the cypress tree to symbolize immortality, God doesn't just symbolize immortality; God is immortal! By likening himself to a green cypress tree, God compared himself to a tree that lived so many more years than a man's lifetime. To man with his short life of eighty years, the cypress tree seemed immortal.

Immortal life is not up to you. You are guaranteed immortality. The question is where you will spend it.

Reference

1. Lockyer, Herbert. *All the parables in the Bible*. Grand Rapids, MI: Zondervan, 1963.

Chapter 12

Among the Myrtle Trees
Zechariah 1:8–13

The parable of the man among the myrtle trees was a prophetic vision, designed to appeal to the eyes rather than the ears. Jews regarded the myrtle as a symbol of something good and beautiful, yet the myrtle tree couldn't compare to the cedar of Lebanon. The parable was set in Judea, an insignificant province of the Persian Empire.

The first year (535–536 BC) the Jews returned to Jerusalem from the Babylonian exile, they rebuilt the temple altar. The second year, they laid the second temple foundation. Non-Jewish people who lived in the area, largely Samaritans, offered to help rebuild the temple. When the Jews refused their assistance, these enemies initiated a systematic program to discourage the Jew's efforts. As a result, temple construction slowed, then stopped for about ten years.

In August 520 BC, God spoke through the Jewish prophet Haggai. God told the Jews to finish building the temple. Haggai identified that the drought in Judea was the result of God's temple remaining in ruins. Although returned Jews built their own homes, they didn't rebuild God's home. Almost immediately, Jews reinitiated temple construction.

Two months after God's message to Haggai, Zechariah started to receive messages from God. Zechariah's prophecies mirrored Haggai's, i.e., rebuild the temple, but included that the Jews repent and serve the Lord. Zechariah was God's prophet for the next forty years (520 to 480 BC).

In the first year of his ministry, Zechariah received eight visions from God in one night. They were visions, not dreams; Zechariah was fully awake. The first vision was a parable that included a plant, the myrtle tree. Here is Zechariah first vision:

> There before me was a man mounted on a red horse. He was standing among the myrtle trees in a ravine. Behind him were red, brown and white horses.
>
> I asked, "What are these, my lord?"
>
> The angel who was talking with me answered, "I will show you what they are."
>
> Then the man standing among the myrtle trees explained, "They are the ones the Lord has sent to go throughout the earth. And they reported to the angel of the Lord who was standing among the myrtle trees, We have gone throughout the earth and found the whole world at rest and in peace."
>
> Then the angel of the Lord said, "Lord Almighty, how long will you withhold mercy from Jerusalem and from the towns of Judah, which you have been angry with these seventy years?"
>
> So the Lord spoke kind and comforting words to the angel who talked with me.
>
> Then the angel who was speaking to me said, "Proclaim this word: This is what the Lord Almighty says: I am very jealous for Jerusalem and Zion, and I am very angry with the nations that feel secure. I was only a little angry, but they went too far with the punishment. Therefore this is what the Lord says: I will return to Jerusalem with mercy, and there my house will be rebuilt. And the measuring line will be stretched out over Jerusalem, declares the Lord Almighty. Proclaim further: This is what the Lord Almighty says: My towns will again overflow with prosperity, and the Lord will again comfort Zion and choose Jerusalem." (Zechariah 1:8–17, NIV)

Prophets were God's voice on earth. They spoke or recorded exactly what God said, rather than paraphrasing or interpreting God's message. When we examine the details of Zechariah's the parable, we see two conversations. One conversation is between Zechariah and an angel. The second conversation is between "the angel of the Lord" (preincarnate Jesus) and God. The parable's setting is a ravine containing myrtle trees.

If you were a postexile Jew living in Jerusalem, how would you respond to Zechariah's parable of the man among the myrtle trees?

1. Would you have been encouraged or discouraged by Zechariah's parable? Explain your answer.

2. Would there have been any part of you that wondered how God could allow Babylon to enact such vicious brutality on the people of Jerusalem? Possibly, Jerusalemites who lived through the siege and the sacking of Jerusalem saw beloved parents or grandparents die or be murdered.

3. Would you have been a) angry with God, b) grateful that God cared about you and your people enough to discipline you, or c) totally confused about God's supposed goodness?

At the time of Zechariah's prophecy, myrtle trees grew wild throughout Judea. The myrtle is an evergreen shrub or small tree. Under optimal conditions myrtle trees grow up to twenty-four feet tall. Usually, the myrtle tree grew under the canopy of taller trees or where taller trees were harvested or destroyed. Using the myrtle tree to symbolize the Jews, meant that both in the present and in the future, the Jews were a small nation. No longer was the Jewish nation comparable to the 120-foot cedar of Lebanon.

Myrtle   Maria Lin

The myrtle leaf is dark green, oval, and pointed. Leaves are fragrant because the leaf tissue contains oil-secreting glands. Myrtle leaves and flowers have attractive scents which are often described as sweet, flowerlike, aromatic, and unique. Like a leaf from the insignificant myrtle tree, Jews could still give off a sweet aroma pleasing to God.

In Zechariah's parable, myrtle trees grew in a ravine. A ravine is a narrow, steep-sided valley, a low place. Myrtle trees don't tolerate shade, yet shade is a common characteristic of a ravine or gorge. Further, myrtle trees are damaged by cold, dry wind, and when young are damaged by frost. In a ravine—the microclimate and setting of Zechariah's parable—young myrtle trees could be damaged by shade, cold, and wind blowing through the ravine. Similarly, the Jewish remnant in Judea could be easily damaged, even destroyed, by conquerors. Future Jewish nations could thrive, but only in the shadow of mighty nations.

The Hebrew word for myrtle tree is *hădaç*.[1] Little is known about the derivation of *hădaç*; however, it may mean "to grow rapidly." In contrast, the word for cedar is *'erez*, meaning "to be firm." Firm means securely or solidly fixed in place and having a structure that resists pressure. The cedar tree was firm because of its tenacious root structure, long life in nature, resistance to insect infestation, and endurance as a building material (see additional characteristics of the cedar tree under The Cedar and Thistle).

Can you think of any advantages of being a myrtle tree rather than a cedar tree?

Like the fast growing myrtle tree, the population in postexile Judea grew rapidly. Some population increase was due to birth rates, but, more probably, Jewish population increased because Jews moved into Judea from other parts of the Persian Empire. With God's assistance the Jews grew again into a nation; however, like the myrtle tree, the Jews didn't have the national durability and firmness seen in King David and Solomon's reigns. The once mighty cedar of Lebanon was gone; it was now a somewhat lowly myrtle tree. Judea was a small province in the outback of the expansive Persian Empire. Going forward, most of Judean history showed that the country was controlled by foreign nations, i.e., Rome, Turkey, Great Britain.

Despite the diminished importance of the Jewish kingdom, Zechariah's parable was a message of hope and encouragement to postexile Jews. The interpretation was that God keeps his promises; God comforted the angel who was distressed about the state of the lives of the postexile Jews. God promised that the Babylonian-Persian Empire would be held accountable for their brutal treatment of his people when Judah and Jerusalem were conquered. Further, God promised that he would return to Jerusalem and Zion with mercy and the temple would be rebuilt.

God promised that people in the tiny Judean province would prosper.

1. The Bible revealed some reasons why people prosper and reasons why they don't prosper in the following verses. Read and summarize reasons for prosperity from these Bible verses:

    a. Deuteronomy 28:62–63

    b. Proverbs 17:20

    c. Proverbs 28:13

2. How can we meld our personal experiences with what the Bible says, yes, even promises, about prosperity being related to a godly life?

3. According to God's word, why have you prospered or not prospered?

a. _____

b. _____

c. _____

Persian Emperor Darius III died about 330 BC, leaving Alexander of Greece ruler of the remaining lands of the once mighty Persian Empire. About two hundred years passed between God consoling the angel of the Lord and God holding the Babylonian-Persian Empire accountable for their brutal treatment of the Jerusalem Jews. Within those two hundred years, Persia fought and lost many battles with vicious enemies where soldiers and civilians were ruthlessly killed. We are reminded anew that God keeps his promises, but God doesn't operate within the same time constraints as man.

**Does God need to return to the United States in a
way similar to his promise to return to Jerusalem?
What would such an event or happening look like?
What is your role in making it happen?**

Reference

1. Strong, James. *The New Strong's exhaustive concordance of the Bible.* Nashville, TN: Thomas Nelson Publishers, 2010.

Section 2

Plants in New Testament Parables

In contrast to the few books written on Old Testament parables, there is an overabundance on New Testament parables. Almost all New Testament parable books focus on Jesus's parables; however, other New Testament figures told parables, e.g., John the Baptist, Paul, James, Peter, and John the Evangelist. Many of these writers used plants to illustrate their spiritual message. Section 2, "Plants in New Testament Parables," contains twelve parables in the New Testament illustrated by plants. Seven parables were given by Jesus and five by other New Testament figures.

The New Testament was written in Greek; the Greek word *parabŏlē* was used for parable.[1] *Parabŏlē* translates as a comparison, a placing beside, and fictitious narrative usually of common life conveying moral truth. Some New Testament truths were comparisons and illustrations presented as simple stories, while others were acted out or seen in visions. Parable development reached its zenith in Jesus's parables; about one-third of his words were parables. But Jesus didn't start his ministry telling parables. Think back to Jesus's Sermon on the Mount. Despite covering several chapters (Matthew 5 to 7), the Sermon contains few parables. Imagine the disciple's surprise when one day Jesus's teaching method changed; he started to teach almost exclusively in parables. The disciples were as confused as the crowds who came to hear Jesus. They asked Jesus why he was using parables.

Jesus used parables for three reasons. First, parables prevented the Jewish leaders—many who were or would become Jesus's enemies—from using his own words to condemn him. Second,

Jesus's use of parables fulfilled Isaiah's prophecy that people wouldn't understand when even the Messiah spoke because they were spiritually dull (Isaiah 6:9–10). Third, parables contained truths that could only be understood through God's revelation. Although God wanted all individuals to understand the parables, the sad truth was some wouldn't understand because they weren't willing to accept Jesus and his message. But to those individuals who were willing to accept Jesus as Messiah, interpretation of parables provided insight into the kingdom of God.

What Jesus taught never seems outdated. Jesus's parables are as relevant as "alerts" that flash on Fox News or CNN. Jesus spoke seven parables in Section 2, but they aren't an exhaustive list of Jesus's parables. They are included because they were the foundation of what Jesus wanted people to know about the kingdom of heaven and because they don't repeat any plant already described in Section 1, "Plants in Old Testament Parables."

Jesus and John the Baptist lived and taught in Galilee, Judea, and in the trans-Jordan area known as Perea. Collectively, these areas are called the Holy Lands. Logically, both thought of plants in their own country when they included plants in parables. Other New Testament parable givers, i.e., Paul, the author of Hebrews, Peter, and John, probably wrote from other parts of Asia Minor or southeastern Europe. Nevertheless, Hebrew scholars and botanists consistently identified Holy Land plants when naming plants used to illustrate their parables.

Reference

1. Strong, James. *The New Strong's exhaustive concordance of the Bible.* Nashville, TN: Thomas Nelson Publishers, 2010.

Chapter 13

John the Baptist and Winnowing Wheat

Matthew 3:12

John the Baptist spoke this parable to foretell actions of the coming Messiah (Christ). John used the familiar agricultural metaphor of separating (winnowing) good grains of wheat from useless chaff. John taught that when Christ comes, he would separate godly believers from those with a superficial or no belief in God. John's parable is about destiny.

In the early part of the first century, residents of Judea and Galilee were fairly prosperous. No wars ravaged these regions which were part of the Roman Empire. Most residents knew how to work within the Roman political and economic systems. The sentiment, "Just keep things level," reflected the self interest and expediency of residents.

Bruce and I stayed for a weekend at a small resort in Canada called Destiny Bay. Over long dinners, we watched humming birds frenetically fly from one feeder to another drinking the nectar.

1. The humming birds were so busy that they never slowed down to think about their destiny. Is their behavior in any way a reflection of yours? Explain your answer.

2. Think about standing before the judgment seat of God. How do you think you will feel?

3. What are you going to say when God asks you to give an account of your behavior here on earth?

A prophet, John the Baptist was born to Zechariah and Elizabeth. His home town was in the hill country of Judea. Zechariah was from the family of Abijah, a division of priests that rotated to Jerusalem to burn daily incense in the temple. Realistically, John followed in Zechariah's footsteps and became the village priest. As a member of Abijah's priestly family, John probably had at least one rotation in the Jerusalem temple prior to his sojourn in the wilderness.

John preached personal acknowledgement and repentance of sins followed by baptism—full body emersion—in water as an outward sign of repentance. The baptismal water symbolically washed sins away. Some Jews recalled the words of the ancient prophets about a coming Messiah. Many yearned for his arrival. When they heard John and saw his actions, they asked John if he was the predicted savior. John answered their question with a firm denial saying that the coming Messiah was mightier than he (Matthew 3:11); John wasn't worthy to take off or carry the sandals of the Messiah. John went on to say that the Messiah will baptize people with the Holy Spirit and with fire.

John didn't stop with his message of repentance and physical act of baptism. John exhorted those baptized to change their behavior and bear fruit consistent with repentance (Luke 3:8–14). When those baptized asked him what they should do, John's answer wasn't that they quit their jobs and follow him; but rather, in their lives and jobs, they should act honorably, treat others fairly, and share with the less fortunate. For example, John told men with two tunics to give one to the man who had none. Soldiers should stop accusing people falsely and extorting money from them.

John the Baptist spoke bluntly to the multitudes who came to him for baptism, but reserved his worst denunciations for Jerusalem's elite, Pharisees, Sadducees, and priests. He called them "vipers" (Luke 3:7). The fierceness of his words suggests John had firsthand knowledge of their behavior. Perhaps, when he rotated through the Jerusalem temple as a priest, John saw the excesses, insincerity, and, yes, even corruption that infected priests of the Herodian-style Jerusalem temple.

**Some individuals believe they are "above"
the need to repent.**

1. Do you think the elite, upper-crust Pharisees, Sadducees, and wealthy Jerusalemites in first century Palestine believed that a country priest/prophet's words applied to them? Why or why not?

2. Why did John label these men as "vipers?"

3. How would you compare most of today's intelligent and talented politicians and pundits to the Pharisees, Sadducees, and Jerusalem leaders who came to see John?

John the Baptist spoke several parables that used plants to make the comparison between the physical reality and spiritual truth, i.e., "the axe is laid to the root of the tree, and every tree that does not produce good fruit will be cut down and thrown into the fire" (Luke 3:9). His parable on winnowing described separating chaff from wheat kernels:

> His winnowing fan (shovel, fork) is in His hand, and He will thoroughly clear out and clean His threshing floor and gather and store His wheat in His barn, but the chaff He will burn up with fire that cannot be put out. (Matthew 3:12, AMP)

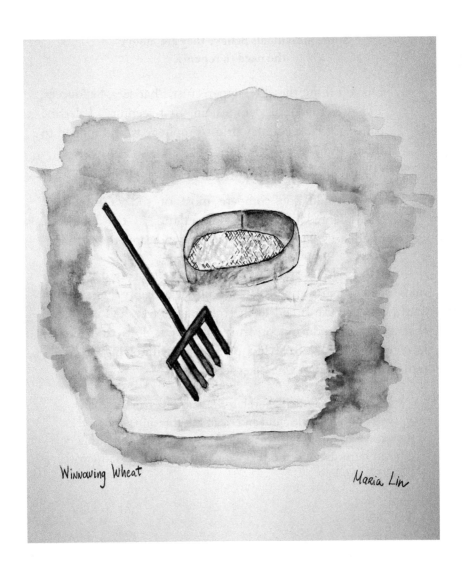

Winnowing Wheat   Maria Lin

In ancient Judea, wheat kernels (seed, grain) were separated from the chaff (stalks, straw) on threshing floors. Generally, chaff was unusable except as fodder for livestock. The farmer separated the wheat kernels from the chaff using a process called winnowing. Winnowing consisted of throwing the threshed material (chaff and grain) into the air with a fork or a flat basket. The wind separated the valuable grains of wheat from the chaff. Because wheat kernels were heavier than chaff, they fell to the ground or back into the basket. The lighter chaff, dirt, etc., were blown away by the wind. At times, farmers used fans to create air currents to blow chaff and other impurities away from the valuable wheat kernels.

Through most Old Testament times, poor Israelites used barley for bread. By the New Testament era, wheat was used for bread, other baking, and cereal. Ancient peoples called wheat the "giving grain" and associated it with the cycle of birth, life, and death. For the ancient Hebrews, wheat symbolized life from God, primarily physical life. For New Testament era people, John could have identified no better plant than wheat to contrast righteous and unrighteous individuals.

From earliest times, man planted wheat because of its high nutritional—life-giving—content. Like barley, wheat was an annual crop; however, wheat required a longer growing season (about one hundred days) than barley. Usually, wheat was harvested May. The longer growing season for wheat than for barley could have reassured John's listeners. John acknowledged that repentance, maturation, and amendment of life take time just as wheat took time to grow. The Presence Bread for the Tabernacle and Temple was made with fine white wheat flour. God had every right to expect that Jews' actions, especially those of Jewish leaders, were pure similar to the purist wheat flour used in Tabernacle bread.

John the Baptist spoke his parable on winnowing wheat soon after starting his ministry. Yet, John's parable demonstrated a sure knowledge of a difference in outcome for the righteous versus the unrighteous. Both the wheat and the chaff had an eternal destination. One was in God's storehouse and the other in unquenchable fire. Perhaps, John the Baptist's words on winnowing wheat and chaff had their origins in Psalm 1:4–5, i.e., the wicked are like chaff that the wind blows away. They won't be able to stand when God judges them. Sinners will be separated from the assembly of the righteous as chaff is separated from wheat kernels.

**Christ is going to thoroughly clear out
and clean his threshing floor.
When Christ is done, the threshing floor will be empty.**

1. Given John's parable, what is going to happen to men and women who are on the fence, who haven't made a decision to follow Jesus?

2. Is there going to be an opportunity for a "do over" when Jesus comes the second time? Explain your answer using verses from the Bible if possible.

3. What will be your destiny when Jesus separates wheat from chaff?

When John the Baptist told the parable of winnowing wheat and chaff, the spiritual reality was that the coming Messiah would distinguish or separate the righteous from the unrighteous. Messiah would critically analyze people's heart, not pious actions. John said that sincere, righteous individuals—wheat kernels—will be taken and stored in the farmer's barn, that is heaven. In contrast, chaff, those with pretend piety, will be forever burned.

**God isn't going to accept any dirt, chaff, or straw
into his barn. Where does that leave you?**

Chapter 14

Harvesting Weeds (Darnel)
Matthew 13:24–30, 36–43

This parable addresses the perplexing presence of evil on the earth by using a series of contrasts, i.e., the good farmer-enemy, wheat-tares, and two harvests. The parable was relevant to first century individuals because it described a common occurrence, wheat and weeds growing in the same field. Simultaneously, the parable was prophetic; it described what will happen at God's final harvest.

**So many parables include—even focus primarily on—
a final outcome or eternity.**

1. Why all these Bible writings, even warnings, allocated to a final outcome for individuals?

2. Do you ever look at celebrities, whether politicians, actors, or pundits, and think that they are attractive and articulate? Do you envy them? Do you ever wonder what their relationship is with God? I've come to believe that I need to pray for, not envy, many of these personalities.

3. Is silence consent? Are we silent about certain social issues because our lives haven't been influenced enough by God's word?

Matthew is the only gospel writer who included Jesus's parable of the weeds. Because Matthew wrote for a primarily Jewish audience, Jews were meant to interpret and apply the parable's content to their lives. Today, Christians can use the parable of the weeds to more fully understand God's actions here on earth.

Chapter 13 begins with Jesus leaving a home where he was staying and taking a seat near the shore of the Sea of Galilee. In ancient times, teachers sat when they taught, rather than standing behind a podium. Tradition locates Jesus's discourse at the "Cove of the Parables," a horseshoe-shaped amphitheater where Jesus's voice could carry to a crowd of hundreds (Matthew 13:1–2, ESV). Because Jesus was teaching in a rural area in Galilee, his audience knew about farming practices to include the damage that weeds do to wheat crops.

Likely, Jesus offered the parable of the weeds late in his first year, but more probably early in his second year of public ministry. By this time scribes and Pharisees started to push back at him. They wanted Jesus to explain his "supposed" authority to teach and to give them a sign to verify his messianic identity. Initially, Jesus spoke the parable of the wheat and weeds to a crowd. Later, he interpreted it for his disciples, but he never interpreted it for the crowds of people who came to listen to his teachings. Here is Christ's parable of the weeds:

> The kingdom of heaven may be compared to a man who sowed good seed in his field, but while his men were sleeping, his enemy came and sowed weeds among the wheat and went away. So when the plants came up and bore grain, then the weeds appeared also. And the servants of the master of the house came and said to him, "Master, did you not sow good seed in your field? How then does it have weeds?" He said to them, "An enemy has done this." So the servants said to him, "Then do you want us to go and gather them?" But he said, "No, lest in gathering the weeds you root up the wheat along with them. Let both grow together until the harvest, and at harvest time I will tell the reapers, Gather the weeds first and bind them in bundles to be burned, but gather the wheat into my barn." (Matthew 13:24–30, ESV)

Darnel

Wheat

Maria Lin

In the parable of the weeds, the weed was most likely darnel, also known as tares and poison ryegrass. Darnel originated in the Mediterranean region including the Middle East. It is distributed widely throughout Israel to include extreme deserts. Like wheat, darnel is an annual plant; it grows in two- to three-foot spikes. Again like wheat, darnel spikes terminate in a grain head; however, the darnel grain head is longer than that of the wheat head and darnel lacks the fuzzy appearance of wheat head. Initially, the darnel plant—stems, leaves, and flowers—is green and looks like wheat. When wheat and darnel are less developed, most farmers can't tell the difference between the two; however, as summer progresses, darnel plants turn black. The black color is a sure way to differentiate darnel from wheat which is creamy brown. Further, when both wheat and darnel are fully mature, wheat stalks are taller than darnel.

Even a few grains of darnel negatively affect wheat crop quality. Darnel seeds are poisonous to people and livestock. Because darnel seeds are similar in appearance, size, and weight to wheat, it is difficult to separate or remove darnel seeds from wheat seeds. Often darnel seeds are contaminated with a variety of crop pests and diseases such as fungus. The best form of invasive species management is prevention, a farmer plants clean wheat seeds. Recently developed herbicides kill darnel; however, in ancient Israel, farmers had no herbicides. They relied on sowing clean seeds to get a clean wheat crop.

The dialogue between the farmer and his servants showed the farmer's knowledge of wheat and darnel seeds and growth patterns of both. Probably, the farmer didn't purchase wheat seeds for planting because bought wheat seeds could be contaminated with darnel. Instead, the farmer used last year's wheat seed from his own fields. He and his servants knew that the wheat seeds they planted didn't contain darnel seeds. The only way fields could be contaminated with darnel was if the darnel seeds were deliberately planted.

When I first read that an enemy contaminated a farmer's wheat fields with weeds, I had a hard time believing the farmer's assertion that an enemy planted weeds in his field. The farmer sounded like he was making an excuse for careless planting of his fields. After investigating agriculture practices in first-century Israel, I learned that jealous farmers often contaminated rivals' fields to discredit the rival farmer and to increase the value of wheat from their own fields.

Most plants need fertilizer. Fertilizer contributes to plant growth and optimal fruit production.

1.   Name some bad fruit (sins) that we produce in our lives. If you need help, read Galatians 5:19–21.

2.   What does the Bible consider good fruit production in our lives? If you need help with this list, read Galatians 5:22–23.

3.   For plants, i.e., wheat, grapes, even weeds, to grow optimally, the soil conditions have to be right. Routinely, gardeners fertilize soil where plants grow. In contrast, often we neglect to fertilize the soil of our lives. What could or should we do to fertilize our walk with Christ?

     a.   _____

     b.   _____

     c.   _____

Several verses after Jesus told the parable of the weeds, he provided the disciples with its interpretation. Here is Jesus's explanation of the parable:

> The one who sows the good seed is the Son of Man. The field is the world, and the good seed is the sons of the kingdom. The weeds are the sons of the evil one, and the

enemy who sowed them is the devil. The harvest is the end of the age, and the reapers are angels. Just as the weeds are gathered and burned with fire, so will it be at the end of the age. The Son of Man will send his angels, and they will gather out of his kingdom all causes of sin and all law-breakers, and throw them into the fiery furnace. In that place there will be weeping and gnashing of teeth. Then the righteous will shine like the sun in the kingdom of their Father. (Matthew 13:35–43, NIV)

Christ affirmed John the Baptist's parable of winnowed wheat when he told the disciples that at the final judgment wheat and weeds would be separated, and the righteous placed in the barn or storehouse of God and the unrighteous thrown into a fiery furnace.

Repeatedly, Scripture writers affirmed that the course of human history is set toward judgment. No human will escape a judgment. Jesus described how weeds came into the world and why they were allowed to grow. The origin of weeds on earth was Satan who sowed them in the pristine fields that God created. Remember, Satan sowed disobedience to God back in the Garden of Eden. Because God doesn't want anyone—any man or woman—to end up in the fiery furnace, he restrains his angels. They aren't allowed to pull out unrighteous evildoers until they mature. When it is abundantly clear that weeds are indeed weeds and not good wheat, angels reap or remove them, not to be placed in the storehouse of the Lord, but to be destroyed.

You have persevered and have endured
hardships for my name.
Yet, I hold this against you:
You have forsaken your first love.
(Revelation 2:3–4, NIV)

1. What should be a Christian's first love?

2. How should we make amendment for forgetting our first love? If you are not sure, read Revelation 2:5.

3. If you repent, amend your life, and return to your first love, what will Christ do for you (Revelation 2:7)?

In Revelation, John described a vision of the earth being harvested (Revelation 14:14–20). Although grapes rather than weeds were harvested; the vision mirrors Christ's parable of the weeds. Angels harvest grapes and throw them into the great winepress of God's wrath. The grapes were trampled and blood flowed outside the press. In this vision, John noted that the winepress was located outside the city. At the final harvest, evildoers aren't in the city wall or in God's barn (storehouse). In contrast, individuals who have a personal relationship with Christ are blessed because their righteous deeds follow them into eternity (Revelation 13:13).

Weeds in my garden keep growing back. My husband tells me to spray them with an herbicide that goes into the plant, travels to the root, and kills it. The problem is that weeds are often intertwined with my beautiful flowers. If I spray the weeds, drops of herbicidal spray may get on flowers and kill them.

Chapter 15

Lily of the Field
Matthew 6:28–30

Jesus's parable of lilies adorning field grass is part of the Sermon on the Mount. Often considered Jesus's inaugural address, the entire sermon is recorded in Matthew 5:1 through Matthew 7:28. In it Jesus explained what he expected of members of his kingdom. This address is the standard for Christian life. The parable is about anxiety and worry.

Anxiety is an extreme uneasiness of mind,
even a brooding fear,
about something that may or may not come to pass.

1. Have you ever felt anxious? What does that feel like to you? According to Proverbs 12:25, how does anxiety affect a person?

2. Isaiah 35:4 tells us what we should do if we see others experiencing anxiety. What is that direction?

3. How can you claim Isaiah's advice in your own life? Consider memorizing Isaiah 35:4 and repeating it out loud when you are experiencing anxiety.

Before the Sermon on the Mount, Jesus was baptized by John. Following his baptism, Jesus fasted for forty days alone in the wilderness. At the end of the forty days, Satan approached Jesus and tempted him with riches beyond measure here on earth if Jesus would worship Satan. Jesus refused and Satan left him. After he heard that King Herod imprisoned John the Baptist, Jesus went to live in Capernaum on the northwest side of the Sea of Galilee. There, Jesus called several disciples and began his teaching and healing ministry.

Jesus was teaching in Galilee synagogues when news of him spread through the area. Large crowds followed him. Seeing the crowds, Jesus went to a mountain and sat down. On the northwestern corner of the Sea of Galilee near Capernaum is a gently sloping hillside, often considered the Sermon location. The hillside would have been covered with grass interspersed with wildflowers. Possibly, Jesus sat at the bottom of the hillside while listeners sat in the grass at higher elevations similar to an amphitheater. Matthew wrote that Jesus's disciples came to him and he began to teach them. Most likely the "them" Matthew identified referred to both Jesus's disciples and the crowds present at that time.

In the Sermon on the Mount, Jesus included the Beatitudes. He spoke about the salt of the earth and warned that if the salt lost its flavor it was good for nothing. Jesus gave God's standards for murder, adultery, divorce, and love of enemies. Matthew recorded that Jesus first spoke the Lord's Prayer in the Sermon on the Mount. In the parable of the lilies and the grass, Jesus seems to chide listeners. His exact words were:

> And why do you worry about clothes? See how the lilies of the field grow. They do not labor or spin. Yet I tell you that not even Solomon in all his splendor was dressed like one of these. If that is how God clothes the grass of the field, which is here today and tomorrow is thrown into the fire, will he not much more clothe you—you of little faith? (Matthew 6:28–30, NIV)

Jesus began this parable by asking listeners why they worried about clothes. In early Galilee, many individuals had no more than one or two sets of clothes. One set was for every day wear and one for festive occasions. Jesus wasn't asking why individuals worried about *which* outfit they wore on a particular day. Instead he asked why they worried *if* they had clothes to wear. Then, Jesus said that King Solomon in his splendor—in his rich, colorful garb—wasn't dressed as gloriously as a lily of the field, a simple field flower. In contrast to peasant's clothes made primarily from wool, goat hair, or camel chair, Solomon's clothes were made of linen, cotton, or silk. Often Solomon's outer mantle or robe was decorated with the fur of exotic animals. Solomon's clothes were usually purple, the symbol of royalty; however, on special occasions, the king wore white garments to denote purity, cleanliness, and joy. Peasant clothes were undyed or dyed brown.

How many separate outfits do you have in your closet?

1. If you stopped buying clothes for yourself for a year, would you be more or less anxious?

2. Estimate the amount of extra money you would save.

3. Imagine giving that money to a fund that provided food and clothing to orphans or widows, e.g., Orphan Medical Network International (OMNI) or Samaritan's Purse. Seriously, how do you think you would feel about making a donation of this size to a Christian charity?

When Christ used the example of lilies, most likely he wasn't referring to the true lily described by the prophet Hosea. Instead, Jesus meant the anemone, a flower that grew wild and abundant in fields, was colorful, and known to most people. Often, anemones are called windflowers because even a gentle breeze will cause them to sway on their thin stalks. Anemones are perennials; they regrow year after year.

In Israel, the anemone blooms December through April. A single flower blooms on a leafless stalk. Normally, flowers have six petals. Most of these field flowers were red; however, anemone blossoms could be white, pink, purple, or blue. Anemone with red petals are most resistant to harsh growing conditions; they abound in Israel's steppes and deserts. Anemone flowers open in the morning and close in the evening. Although anemones have no nectar, flowers attract beetles and bees that feed on pollen.

The anemone has been associated with the Trinity, sorrow, and death; however, in the Sermon on the Mountain, the parable was about worry or anxiety. Three times in the Matthew 6:25–34 passage, Jesus told listeners not to worry. Specifically, Jesus identified four things they shouldn't worry about—their life, what they would eat, what they would drink, and what they would wear. Jesus promised that God knows his children's needs and God will meet those needs. Pragmatically, Jesus asked, "Who by worrying can add a single hour to his life" (Matthew 6:27, NIV)?

Stop reading right now! Go back and reread Jesus's question: can you add a single hour to your life, can you change a single outcome, can you increase or decrease what you have or don't have by worrying? My aunt was a worrier, but she didn't just worry in her own mind, she worried out loud. We all heard her anxieties, her concerns, and her dour predictions which worry generated. She lived a life of "what if." What if this happens, what if that happens. As a young girl, I didn't like to be around her. I didn't want to hear about all of the negative things that could happen. No, I'm not recommending that we keep our heads in the sand, so to speak; however, remember the old saying that we don't need to borrow trouble by speculating about what could happen.

**Which of you by being anxious can add a
single hour to his life span? (Luke 12:25, ESV)**

1. By asking this question, what conclusion was Jesus trying to lead his listeners to? In other words, interpret Jesus's parable for your own life.

2. How are you (not could you!) applying the parable of the anemone to your life?

Have you ever seen wildflowers growing in a meadow as you drove along a little-used road? I have, and wondered why all this beauty was there. Why did God put beautiful flowers amidst this grass when so few people see them? Perhaps the answer is that God made the beauty for just one human—me(!), as I viewed it. On the other hand, perhaps God put the vibrant wildflowers in grassy meadows to remind himself that he knows every blade of grass, every flower, and every human.

To my timeframe, wildflowers are transient.
In God's timeframe, I am transient.
Why am I important or unimportant to God?

Chapter 16

Growth of a Mustard Seed
Mark 4:30–32

Jesus seemed to like the mustard seed. He used it several times to illustrate parables and teachings. The current parable was about the kingdom of God. This parable appeared in Matthew, Mark, and Luke. In Matthew it was placed between the parable of the weeds and Jesus's explanation of that parable.

Jesus was in Galilee when he told the parable of the mustard seed. Because Jesus grew up in a small village, he was aware of plants, their growth patterns, and their uses. He knew that mustard seeds are one of the smallest of all seeds, yet this tiny seed grows into a tree big enough that birds perch on its branches. Here's how Mark recorded Jesus's parable:

> What shall we say the kingdom of God is like, or what parable shall we use to describe it? It is like a mustard seed, which is the smallest seed you plant in the ground. Yet when planted, it grows and becomes the largest of all garden plants, with such big branches that the birds of the air can perch in its shade. (Mark 4:30–32, NIV)

Jesus used several parables to characterize the kingdom of God, e.g., the sower, wheat and tares, and leaven. This particular one illustrated the growth and expansion of God's kingdom on the earth. Although the church began in Judea, a small province of the Roman Empire, it grew rapidly to become larger than the mightiest empire on earth. The parable was prophetic; Jesus described what was to occur in the future.

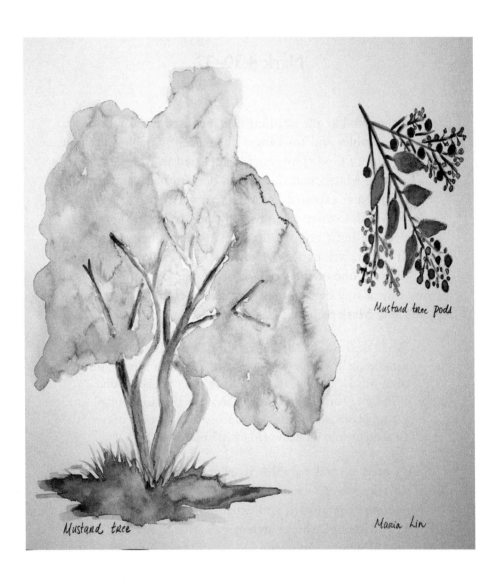

Mustard tree pods

Mustard tree

Maria Lin

**The growth of the Christian church was inevitable.
Jesus said it would happen.**

1. What direction did Jesus give to his disciples to grow the church? If you aren't sure, read the following verses, then, answer the question.

    a. Mark 16:15

    b. Matthew 28:19

    c. Acts 1:8

In African and Middle Eastern countries, the mustard tree is called the toothbrush tree. Indigenous to Persia (Iran), the mustard tree could have moved into Palestine along trade routes. Alternatively, returning Jewish exiles may have brought tiny mustard tree seeds back from Persia and planted them in gardens and fields. It is an evergreen shrub or tree that grows to twenty feet. Often the mustard tree's many branches start low to the ground so that mustard trees grow as wide as tall. Mustard trees grow quickly and reach full size in a few years.

The mustard tree's growth pattern illustrated how the Christian church would grow. Like the branches of a mustard tree, Christianity spread wide—that is, over the Roman Empire and even into India and Ethiopia. Similar to the fast growth of a mustard tree, Christianity flooded the ancient world. In a few centuries Christianity went from unheard of, to being outlawed, to the official religion of an empire. Many powerful men attempted to stop the spread of "The Way," the early name for the Christian church. The Jerusalem Jewish leadership tried to stop it when they arrested Jesus and turned him over to Pilate for crucifixion. Herod attempted to stifle the teaching of the apostles when he killed the apostle James and had Peter arrested. Roman emperor's murdered believers in arenas. Paul was beaten, confined to house arrest, jailed, and finally murdered; however, his letters—many written when he was confined or jailed—formed the backbone of the spread of the good news of Jesus to the Gentile world. Jesus's parable of the mustard seed came true in the early centuries of the first millennia after Jesus's death.

Use Mark 16:15, Matthew 28:19, and Acts 1:8 and answer the next three questions.

1. It is the twenty-first century. Do Christians today need to spread the good news of Christ?

2. What is the difference between being a witness of Christ with your words and with your behavior?

3. There was an obituary about a woman that said she belong to x Christian church and was active in y and z Christian activities. A colleague told me that she worked with the woman every day for twenty-three years and didn't know she was a Christian. How would you feel if someone said that about you?

Mustard trees were used for shade because of their low-growing branches. Similarly, people from all nations took refuge under the canopy of Christianity. Unlike Jotham's thornbush, the mustard tree had no thorns to deter people from resting beneath it. Although wild animals sometimes fed on tree shoots, many branches grew tall enough that predators couldn't reach birds that sat on them. Think back on the Egyptian, Greek, and Roman empires. Each culture had so many gods and goddesses that it was almost impossible to remember who was who and who did what. Yet, I don't know any stories where a god died for the sins of a believer or individuals who weren't yet believers. In contrast, the Christian religion has one God. God's son came to live on earth and then died for the sins of each man, woman, and child on earth at that time and for those who would be born in the future. Like a mustard tree providing shade to people and livestock, Christianity wants to provide shade and protection for every individual on earth.

In Jesus's parable of the mustard tree, birds settled in its branches. Some Bible commentators took this clause as a warning to keep the early Christian church pure. In the ancient Near East, the phrase "birds of the air" was used to symbolize demonic forces in Scripture. When Jesus noted that birds settled in the mustard tree branches, he may have been warning disciples that Satan would attempt to encroach into the Kingdom of God. Certainly, Jesus's warning became reality. Jews (Judaizers) advocated that newly converted Christians could be justified only by observing Jewish laws such as circumcision and adherence to dietary laws. Further, Gnostics claimed to possess a secret knowledge, a "higher truth." The higher knowledge was acquired not from the Bible or the apostles' teachings, but from a higher mystical plain of existence. Individuals with this special knowledge, for example, Jezebel in the Thyatiran church, believed they were elevated above other Christians because of their deeper knowledge of God (Revelation 2:18–25).

Importantly, the parable of the mustard seed remains true in the twenty-first century. Even with the anti-Christian rhetoric of today and many churches turning from God's commandments, continuation—even extension—of the church Jesus founded is inevitable. My minister believes that the twenty-first century is more like the first century church than any other century in time. The Roman Empire and western civilizations are similar. Like the first-century Roman Empire, westernized society embraces varied religious beliefs along with situational ethics and values. In the Roman Empire, Christian believers were under attack from nonbelievers and civil authorities alike. Today, claiming to be a Christian in western society causes ridicule and subtle, and not so subtle, persecution. Often first-century Christians were, and twenty-first-century Christians are, required by law to participate in actions that conflict with their faith.

Throughout the Roman Empire, men, women, and children were persecuted and murdered because they acknowledge Christ as their Lord. Have you ever wondered why first-century Christians, who suffered so severely for their faith, still remained believers and refused to deny they were Christians? I asked myself that question. Then, I recalled a recent television news clip in which twenty Christian men were beheaded with the beauty of the Mediterranean Sea as the backdrop. Their crime was belief in Jesus; they refused to deny Jesus and convert to another religion. These men were no different than individuals in the first- and second-century Roman Empire. The second-century Church father Tertullian wrote that "the blood of martyrs is the seed of the Church." Seeing a person stand firm in their faith despite slander, persecution, and even death often causes onlookers to investigate that faith. Some come to a believing knowledge of Jesus. Thereby, more individuals rest under the canopy of the Christian church.

It is inevitable that Christians will be persecuted for their righteous behavior.

1. Read Matthew 5:10. What did Jesus say about being persecuted for righteous behavior? Was Jesus ever persecuted for his own righteous behavior?

2. Often we don't recognize religious persecution. We believe that people are unkind because of some quirk in our personality. Don't be so quick to blame yourself when you are persecuted. Consider that you are being persecuted for your righteous behavior/standing for God.

3. Identify two to three situations where you were persecuted for your personal righteous behavior.

   a. _____

   b. _____

   c. _____

At this time in the life of the Christian faith, it seems to be spreading more in developing countries (Africa, South America, Asia) than in westernized countries. Important for Christians is the answer to the question, "Where will Christianity inevitably spread and grow even deeper roots?" Will it be in Greece, Rome, or Spain, where Christianity was first embraced; perhaps Germany and Great Britain, homes to great reformation thought? What about the United States, founded on principles of religious liberty? We need to pray that all countries experience revival in Christian thought so more individuals can rest in the shade of God's love.

All Christians have a role to play in continuing and extending Jesus's church. Are you engaged in the role Jesus identified for you?

Chapter 17

Moving a Mulberry Tree
Luke 17:6

In a parable about a mulberry tree, Jesus alluded to the power of faith. Although Matthew, Mark, and Luke recorded several of Jesus's teachings on faith, this one-verse parable was recorded only by Luke. Most likely Peter told it to Luke.

**"Now faith is being sure of what we hope for
and certain of what we do not see." (Hebrew 11:1, NIV)**

1. Write down your definition of faith; the faith that you have, not an idealized version.

2. Look up the following verses about faith:

   a. Romans 1:17

   b. 2 Corinthians 5:7

   c. Hebrews 11:6

   d. 1 Peter 1:7–9

3. Write down your definition of faith. How did it change from question #1 to question #3?

When Jesus spoke the parable of the mulberry tree, he was talking privately to his disciples. Jesus outlined responsibilities for Christian discipleship. One responsibility was to never lead a person into sin. Jesus said it would be better for a disciple to be thrown into the sea with a millstone tied around his neck than to cause another to sin. A second responsibility was to rebuke a brother if he sins. The third responsibility—and perhaps the hardest—was to forgive a brother if he repents of sin and asks for forgiveness, even as often as seven times a day. Seven times a day meant that the repentance-forgiveness cycle was limitless.

After hearing these requirements, disciples were overwhelmed with responsibilities as followers of Jesus. How could they live so blameless a life that they never caused another individual to sin? Did they have the courage to rebuke a fellow Christian when he or she sinned? How could they, simple men that they were, forgive and forgive and forgive? In desperation, the disciples cried out to Jesus, "Increase our faith!" (Luke 17:5, NIV). The disciples wanted greater faith to live up to the standards Jesus set. Jesus gave them a one sentence response:

> If you have faith as small as a mustard seed, you can say to this mulberry tree, "Be uprooted and planted in the sea," and it will obey you. (Luke 17:6, NIV)

The Greek word for faith used in this parable is *pistis*, which means moral conviction and reliance on Christ for salvation.[1] Also, *pistis* has a more abstract definition which includes "consistency." By using *pistis*, Jesus told disciples they could meet the responsibilities that he outlined through consistent reliance on him.

Most of us have faith in something.

1. Name some things or beings that you have faith in?

2. How do you exhibit this faith? In other words how do you act on your faith in these things or people?

3. How is having faith in the person of Jesus different from having faith in your church or your church doctrine?

Have you ever wondered why Jesus used a mulberry tree to illustrate the outcome of a small amount of consistent faith? If I wanted to illustrate the role of faith to move a tree, I would have used the largest tree I knew of, i.e., a cedar or the Tabor oak. Most likely, Jesus chose a mulberry tree because one was nearby. Jesus said, "This mulberry tree," from which we can surmise that Jesus and his disciples were sitting under a mulberry tree or could see one from where they were seated.

The mulberry tree is also called the black mulberry and sycamine tree. In Israel, mulberry tree remains were found that dated from the late Iron Age.[2] Mulberry trees are popular in areas with long, hot summers to include areas of drought. The mulberry tree can reach a height of thirty-three feet, but most times it is shorter. It has a short, stout trunk and a broad canopy. Mulberry trees grew throughout Judea and Galilee. Finding Jesus and disciples sitting under a mulberry tree is consistent with the tree's characteristics and growth pattern. During our stay at Kibbutz Lotan in the southern Negev Desert area, we saw a twenty-five-foot tall mulberry tree which was planted for shade.

Unlike many plant flowers, mulberry tree flowers are one sex or bisexual; sometimes flowers have been known to change from one sex to another. Mulberry trees were domesticated for their fruit, yet trees don't bear much fruit before they are fifteen years of age. Once fruiting starts, trees produces fruit for hundreds of years. Frequently, older mulberry trees produce better tasting fruit than younger trees. In the same way that a mulberry tree produces better-tasting fruit with age, so Christians are more spiritually productive after several (or many) years of studying God's word.

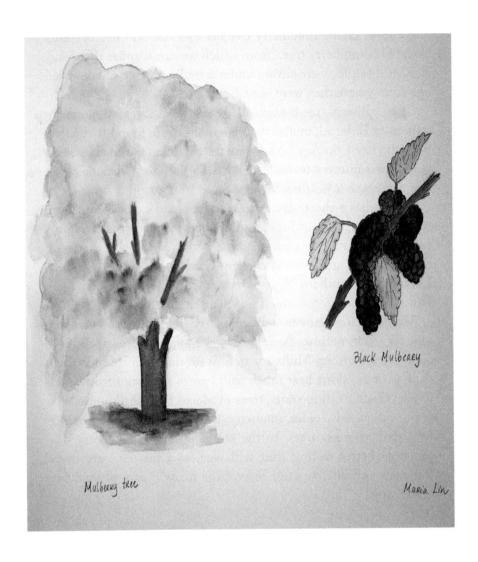

Mulberry tree

Black Mulberry

Maria Lin

The genus name of the mulberry is derived from *mora* (Latin) meaning "delay," probably referring to the mulberry tree being the last tree to bud in the spring. Because the mulberry waits until all possibility of frost is past, it is called the "wisest of all trees." When his disciples asked Jesus to increase their faith, his response was that they could and would accomplish great tasks with a consistent small amount of faith in him. At that point in their walk with Jesus, probably the disciples didn't have unswerving faith in him. They were still getting to know Jesus and coming to realize that he was the promised Messiah. Jesus was wise enough to meet the disciples where they were in their awareness of him.

Because mulberry tree flowers are the last to bloom in the spring doesn't mean that they bloom late. Mulberry flowers bloom at just the right time to be fertile, pollinated, and produce mulberries each year. Have you ever noticed how God seems to time everything, i.e., events, relationships, etc., perfectly? A minister once told his congregation that "God is rarely early, but he is never late." Back when Jesus told his disciples if they have as much faith as a mustard seed, they could move a mulberry tree, in essence Jesus was telling them: "You only need a little faith in me now." What Jesus didn't tell them was that later, when he was arrested, crucified, and murdered, that was the time they would needed a lot of faith in him.

Does size matter?

1. If you have to differentiate between a little faith and a lot of faith, how would you go about making that measurement?

2. Should you wait until your faith in Jesus is large, or fully matured, until you attempt to do something for Jesus, that is, you step out in faith? Why or why not?

3. How is it possible to have a lot of faith on one topic, for instance believing that Christ is the Savior of the world,

while having only a little faith on another topic, i.e., if I tithe on my income before taxes, I will have enough money to pay my bills.

My husband and I had a long talk about consistent reliance on Jesus. Reliance means to be dependent because you have confidence based on experience. Reliance on Jesus doesn't come easy in today's society. We hear that religion is a crutch, as if we would fall down without religion. I'm not sure whether religion is or isn't a crutch for others, but I know that consistently relying on God isn't a crutch for me. It is the smartest thing I've ever done. Been there, done that, tried to live without Jesus at the center of my life. That time in my life was a total disaster. Talk about pain and mistakes! Bruce said the same thing, i.e., before Jesus his life was out of control. After Jesus, reading the Bible, and implementing the Bible's guidelines for living, his life turned around. Our thoughts and lives didn't turn around all at once. Only as we spent consistently more time with God and developed the mind of Jesus did our behavior change. Now, we both intentionally and consistently put Jesus first in our lives, probably because we both have experienced what happened when we put ourselves first.

Is faith logical? Is faith wishful thinking? Is faith the same as hope? What in the world is faith and why is it okay for me to only have a small amount when I tackle a God-given task?

References

1. Strong, James. *The New Strong's exhaustive concordance of the Bible.* Nashville, TN: Thomas Nelson Publishers, 2010.

2. Borowski, Oded. *Agriculture in iron age Israel.* Winona Lake, IN: Eisenbrauns, 2009.

Chapter 18

Reeds Shaken by the Wind
Luke 7:18–28

John the Baptist's public ministry lasted only one to two years. Then, Herod Antipas arrested him. John was imprisoned at Machaerus, a fortress for political prisoners. Jesus contrasted John's firm convictions with reeds blown by the wind.

Ponder the notion of firmness of convictions.

1. What is a conviction? Look up the word in a dictionary if you need to. List four of your convictions.

    a.

    b.

    c.

    d.

2. Is it possible to have a conviction that you don't hold to firmly? In the above list, highlight or check the ones that you don't firmly hold to.

3. Look at the remaining convictions. If you believe them and hold firmly to them, how has your belief changed your life?

Jesus went to John to be baptized. Although this baptism was the start of Jesus's public ministry, it was the high point of John's. Soon afterward, King Herod had John arrested and imprisoned. When Herod arrested John, the ostensible reason was that John criticized Herod for divorcing his powerful Nabatean queen to marry his sister-in-law, Herodias. Personally, Herod was indignant that John had the audacity to hold him—a king—to the same moral standards as everyone else.

The Bible recorded that King Herod used this personal reason for imprisoning John; however, getting John out of circulation made political sense. When John told individuals who came to him for baptism that they must change their behavior, he demanded changes that impacted King Herod's income. For example, John told tax collectors to collect only the amount of money required by Rome. They should stop lining their pockets and those of King Herod by overtaxing citizens. Likewise, soldiers must be content with their pay and stop extorting money from the people of the land. John had tremendous influence with people in Herod's kingdom. According to Josephus, Herod feared that John, with his widespread support from the common people, would instigate rebellion against him.[1]

Compare and contrast John the Baptist and Jesus.

1. Consider how the two of them dressed, where they lived, who their friends were, the manner in which they spoke, etc.

2. Compare the behavior of the civil and religious authorities toward each man.

3. Today, in America, how do you think that we would treat John the Baptist? How would we treat Christ if he lived today?

After John was in prison perhaps fifteen-to-eighteen months, he sent two disciples to Jesus. They asked Jesus if he was the expected Messiah or if they should wait for someone else (Luke 7:19). Jesus didn't give the disciples a direct yes or no answer. Instead, Jesus told the disciples to go back to John and report what they saw and heard, i.e., the blind received their sight, the lame walked, and lepers were cured. After John's messengers left, Jesus asked the crowd what they expected when they went to see John in the desert. In his questioning, Christ told a parable in which he contrasted John the Baptist's behavior with a reed that blew in the wind, swaying first one way than another. Here is how Luke recorded Jesus's parable:

> What did you go out into the desert to see? A reed swayed by the wind? If not, what did you go out to see? A man dressed in fine clothes? No, those who wear expensive clothes and indulge in luxury are in palaces. But what did you go out to see? A prophet? Yes, I tell you, and more than a prophet. This is the one about whom it is written: "I will send my messenger ahead of you, who will prepare your way before you." I tell you, among those born of women there is no one greater than John; yet the one who is least in the kingdom of God is greater than he. (Luke 7:24–28, NIV)

The reed that Jesus referred to when talking about John was the Israeli reed, sometimes called the giant reed and Cypress cane. Reed colonies were located on the banks of natural water courses, in floodplains of medium- or large-sized streams, and in dry riverbanks far from permanent water sources. Reeds grew throughout Israel from Mount Hermon to the Negev Desert.

The giant reed is a perennial; it comes up year after year. Reeds can grow to twenty feet and may grow ten-to-twelve feet in a single growing season. The central reed stalk is called a culm. Culms are about one and a half inches in diameter and hollow. Each culm has leaves that resemble those on corn stalks; however, leaves have sharp edges that can cut fingers. As drier weather prevails, foliage turns light brown and rattles in the wind. Giant reeds bend with the wind, even when they grow in large colonies. In ancient times, and even today, reeds were used as windbreaks and to stop soil erosion.

Israeli Reed

Maria Lin

Individuals who came to John for baptism knew about reeds; they saw reeds growing along the Jordan River. To them reeds elicited mainly positive thoughts. Probably, they remembered how Isaiah associated reeds with humility (Isaiah 58:5). But Jesus denied that John was similar to a swaying reed. Instead, John was firm and upright. Jesus averred that John's beliefs were certain and John lived by them. John stayed on message (repentance) and on task, (baptism). John didn't have a politically correct bone in his body. He didn't pander to public opinion, giving one message to common people and a second one to the rich and powerful. John called the Jerusalem elite "a brood of vipers." Nor was John silent when King Herod divorced his first wife, Phasaelis, in order to marry his brother's wife.

Although Christ denied that John was a swaying reed, John's purpose reflected how reeds were used in ancient Judea and Galilee. By his words and life, John stood against the erosion of godly behavior. He called ordinary citizens, tax collectors, and civil and religious leaders to change their lives to reflect God's standards. Also, like reeds used as windbreaks, John stood as a buffer between people who were righteous and the secular society of the Roman Empire. The best windbreaks lower wind chill in man, animals, and plants. Everything we know about John the Baptist shows a priest and prophet who lived close to God. As a windbreak, John lowered the chilling effects of a secular Roman society on inhabitants of Galilee and Judea.

The spiritual interpretation of Jesus's parable included an eulogy for John. In addition to commendatory words given at a memorial service, eulogy means "high praise." King Herod had not yet murdered John; however, Jesus eulogized John by saying of all the men (and by extension women) born of woman, there was none greater than John the Baptist. John was no weak reed, or as we would say in modern times, "no shrinking violet."

What do you want in your eulogy?

1. List several characteristics you want to be remembered for, i.e., you were a woman of character, you were a man who loved his family, you were loyal, etc.

2. Now that you have identified what you want to be remembered for, what do you think will be said in your eulogy?

3. Starting today, what can you change about yourself to make your eulogy be what you would like it to be?

Given Jesus's evaluation and high words of praise of John the Baptist, have you ever wondered why religious leaders don't spend more time writing and speaking about John's life?

Reference

1. Whiston, William. *The Works of Josephus, Complete and Unabridged.* Peabody, MA, Hendrickson Publishers Inc., 1987.

Chapter 19

Lost Son and Carob Pods
Luke 15:11–32

The parable of the lost son is one of Jesus's longer parables. It was the last of three parables in which Jesus made the point that God searches for the lost. In the parable, plant pods were mentioned, seemingly in passing; however, the pods played a role in incentivizing the lost son to return home to his father. For years, the parable of the lost son was called the parable of the prodigal son. Prodigal means a person who spends lavishly or foolishly or returns after an absence. Both titles reflect the younger son's behavior.

**Who have you always identified with in this parable—
the older or younger son?**

The context for the parable of the lost son is vital to understanding and interpreting it. At the time a large crowd was following Jesus as he traveled from Galilee southward to Jerusalem. Some in the crowd believed what Jesus taught; others wanted to see him perform a great miracle. Pharisees traveled in the group. Carefully, they watched Jesus's behavior and listened to what he said to learn if he did or said anything that contradicted Jewish law. Pharisee means loyal to God and separated one; however, Pharisee's behavior didn't reflect their name. They were extremists in adhering to a limited portion of the Hebrew law, while ignoring the remainder of it. Pharisees were the most influential Jewish group in Palestine and the most bitter and deadly opponents of Jesus and his message.

At this particular time, Luke recorded that tax collectors and other sinners gathered around Jesus. The Pharisees and teachers of the law started to mutter that Jesus welcomed sinners and even ate with them. In response, Jesus told three parables. The first two were relatively short and focused on a man who lost a sheep and a woman who lost a silver coin. Both items were valuable and owners searched diligently for them. When found, their owners rejoiced. Probably, the tax collectors, sinners, and Pharisees all nodded when they heard Jesus tell these two parables. Correctly, they interpreted the parables to mean that God searches for the lost; however, Jesus's third parable—the parable of the lost son—had a different ending. Here is what Jesus said:

> There was a man who had two sons. The younger one said to his father, "Father, give me my share of the estate."
>
> So he divided his property between them. Not long after that, the younger son got together all he had, set off for a distant country and there squandered his wealth in wild living. After he had spent everything, there was a severe famine in that whole country, and he began to be in need. So he went and hired himself out to a citizen of that country, who sent him to his fields to feed pigs. He longed to fill his stomach with the pods that the pigs were eating, but no one gave him anything.
>
> When he came to his senses, he said, "How many of my father's hired men have food to spare, and here I am starving to death! I will set out and go back to my father and say to him: 'Father, I have sinned against heaven and against you. I am no longer worthy to be called your son; make me like one of your hired men.'" Luke 15:11-19, NIV

Substitute means to exchange, switch, or replace with something else.

1. Substitute is what the younger son did in this parable. He substituted his life as a valued son for a life of shameful living and feeding pigs. He replaced eating the best foods with longing to have carob pods to eat. He planned to ask

his father to let him return home, substituting his role as son for that of a hired hand. If you were the father, what would you think about this son?

2. Often we hear or read that Jesus was the substitute for the sins of many (men and women). What does that even mean? How does that work for me and you as individuals? Was Jesus really the substitute for my individual sin? Did he receive what I should receive?

3. Why would Jesus want to do that? What if I tell Jesus not to bother, that I am okay on my own, like the Pharisees thought their righteousness met God's requirements for salvation? Am I really okay on my own?

> So he got up and went to his father. But while he was still a long way off, his father saw him and was filled with compassion for him; he ran to his son, threw his arms around him and kissed him. The son said to him, "Father, I have sinned against heaven and against you. I am no longer worthy to be called your son."
>
> But the father said to his servants, "Quick! Bring the best robe and put it on him. Put a ring on his finger and sandals on his feet. Bring the fattened calf and kill it. Let's have a feast and celebrate. For this son of mine was dead and is alive again; he was lost and is found." So they began to celebrate. (Luke 15:20-24, NIV)

So far, so good! The parable sounded the same as that of the lost sheep and lost coin. Listening tax collectors and sinners, who identified with the younger son, rejoiced to hear that God forgave them unconditionally. Even the Pharisees and teachers of the law had no criticism of Jesus's words at this point. They believed that repentant sinners could be restored to full fellowship with God. If Jesus had stopped there, all would have been well. What Jesus said next offended and further alienated the Pharisees. Here are Jesus exact words as recorded by Luke:

Meanwhile, the older son was in the field. When he came near the house, he heard music and dancing. So he called one of the servants and asked him what was going on.

"Your brother has come," he replied, "and your father has killed the fattened calf because he has him back safe and sound."

The older brother became angry and refused to go in. So his father went out and pleaded with him. But he answered his father, "Look! All these years I've been slaving for you and never disobeyed your orders. Yet you never gave me even a young goat so I could celebrate with my friends. But when this son of yours who has squandered your property with prostitutes comes home, you kill the fattened calf for him!"

"My son," the father said, "you are always with me, and everything I have is yours." But we had to celebrate and be glad, because this brother of yours was dead and is alive again; he was lost and is found." (Luke 15:25–32, NIV)

When Jesus finished the parable, listeners knew that the older brother was the Pharisees. Jesus's parable exposed the Pharisees for what they were, i.e., hardhearted, self-righteous prigs, who believed that their lifestyle earned them special merit before Father God. In their opinion, everything they did was right. God was happy to have them as believers and would welcome them into his kingdom. Similar to the older son looking down on the younger, Pharisees looked down on tax collectors, prostitutes, and sinners. Pharisees had no awareness of their need for a savior. Their high opinion of themselves wouldn't let them believe that Jesus considered them spiritually impoverished.

The pods that the unrepentant son longed to eat were carob pods, the fruit of the carob tree. Likely, carob trees were brought from Babylon by Jewish exiles when they returned to Judea. In ancient Israel, carob trees were also called John's bread and locust. When John the Baptists lived in the wilderness, he ate locust and wild honey. Possibly, he ate carob pods rather than locust insects. Carob trees grew wild throughout Palestine to include in desert areas.

Carob branch   Maria Lin

Carob trees were small; typically, they grew to thirty-three feet. Leaves are evergreen. Carob pods contain a soft pale-brown pulp and ten-to-thirteen flat, hard seeds. When the fruit is fully ripe and dry, pods are light to dark brown and seeds rattle in the pod. Before winter rains, pods are picked from trees or shaken loose from limbs using a long pole with a terminal hook. In Bible times, pods were used to feed livestock. Carob trees produced pods even in time of drought and famine.

In Jesus's parable, the Gentile farmer didn't give food to the pig keeper. The young man was so hungry that he longed to fill his stomach with the carob pods fed to the pigs. Probably, he didn't eat carob pods because he believed that carobs were fodder for animals, not food for man. In reality, the young man could have eaten both the carob pods and seeds. Today, carob pods are dried, roasted, and ground into carob flour. Often the flour or powder is a substitute for chocolate. Carob pods are naturally sweet, low in fat, high in fiber, contain calcium, and unlike chocolate have no caffeine. Carob pods are used as a thickener in bakery goods, ice cream, and salad dressings. In May at a kibbutz in the southern Negev Desert, I ate a ripe carob pod left on a tree from the previous autumn. It was fibrous and tasted sweet, a little like cocoa.

**What does it take in our lives to cause us to
reach out to God and admit we need his help?**

1. In the story of the lost son, do you think the son would have returned to his father if he had sufficient food to eat at his job feeding pigs?

2. Do you think it's fair for a person who lied and cheated all his life to turn to God in the final days or hours of his life and be saved?

3. Consider the thief on the cross. Aren't you annoyed, just a little bit annoyed, that the thief is going to go to heaven after how he acted most of his life?

I wonder if the Pharisees ever had an experience similar to the younger son's. Likely, they never went hungry. They never found themselves so destitute that they hired themselves out to feed a Gentile's pigs. Mosaic Law declared that swine were unclean (Deuteronomy 14:8). Tending pigs was a degrading activity for an Israelite man. Yet, hunger, despair, absence of self esteem, and not knowing that God welcomes repentant sons and daughters with open arms caused the younger son, and causes many individuals today, to feed pigs rather than eat at God's banquet table.

When the younger son asked the father for his inheritance, in essence he told his father, "I wish you were dead." When we turn away from God to pursue our own desires, we tell God, "You are dead to me." Have you ever done that?

Chapter 20

Virgins with Oil Lamps
Matthew 25:1–13

The parable of ten virgins emphasizes the importance of being prepared for Jesus to return to earth the second time. Preparation includes planning. For the ten young virgins, preparation included having sufficient olive oil to fuel their lamps. Last spring, I sold my Christian books at a "Prepper's Convention." Vendors were selling everything imaginable to prepare buyers for natural or manmade disasters, i.e., dried food, batteries, small stoves, guns, and ammunition. Seeing the hundreds of participants caused me to think about Jesus's second coming and preparation for it. If all these individuals could prepare for disaster, surely I could prepare for the greatest future event ever to occur, the second coming of Jesus.

Christians must prepare their minds for action!

1. When Peter exhorted individuals in the scattered Christian church to prepare their minds for action (1 Peter 1:13–16), he wasn't recommending a contemplative lifestyle, i.e, attending a Bible study, or listening to Christian radio. Peter expected action from Christians as they waited for Jesus to come. Read 1 Peter 1:13-16, what did Peter expect Christians to do?

   a.

   b.

   c.

   d.

Beginning with Adam and Eve, God-fearing individuals looked for a coming Messiah. Abraham and about five hundred years later Moses believed that God would send the Messiah. As years turned into decades, decades to centuries, and centuries to millennium, many Jews believed that the notion of a coming Messiah was a myth. The last prophet in the Old Testament, Malachi (440–430 BC), recorded a hypothetical conversation between men of Israel (Malachi 3:13–18). One group identified that it was futile to serve God and carry out his requirements. Arrogant evildoers prospered. The redemption (Messiah) that good men looked for had not appeared even after many centuries. Another group of men feared and followed God. God wrote their names in a scroll of remembrance, similar to a record of notable deeds kept by earthly kings (Esther 6:1–6, Isaiah 4:3). God promised that on judgment day these men would be spared and separated from men who didn't serve him.

Jesus told the parable of the ten virgins to his disciples to reinforce Malachi's teaching. At the time Jesus was seated on the Mount of Olives. It was Passover week. In a few days, Jerusalem's Jewish leaders would capture Jesus, turn him over to Pilate, and demand that the Romans crucify him. Here is the parable:

> The kingdom of heaven will be like ten virgins who took their lamps and went out to meet the bridegroom. Five of them were foolish and five were wise. The foolish ones took their lamps but did not take any oil with them. The wise, however, took oil in jars along with their lamps. The bridegroom was a long time in coming, and they all became drowsy and fell asleep. At midnight the cry rang out: "Here's the bridegroom! Come out to meet him!" Then all the virgins woke up and trimmed their lamps.
>
> The foolish ones said to the wise, "Give us some of your oil; our lamps are going out."
>
> "No," they replied, "there may not be enough for both us and you. Instead, go to those who sell oil and buy some for yourselves."

But while they were on their way to buy the oil, the bridegroom arrived. The virgins who were ready went in with him to the wedding banquet. And the door was shut. Later the others also came. "Sir! Sir!" they said. "Open the door for us!"

But he replied, "I tell you the truth, I don't know you." Therefore keep watch, because you do not know the day or the hour. (Matthew 25:1–13, NIV)

The plant identified in the parable of the virgins was the olive tree. Olive oil fueled the lamps of the waiting virgins. The olive tree is one of the world's oldest cultivated trees. The olive tree is indigenous to present day Israel and Syria. Its dry composition makes the olive tree drought-tolerant. Olive trees live up to one thousand years. Very old trees can be hollow, secondary to fungus having attacked the wood. Leaves appear gray-green on top, while the bottom has a silvery appearance.

The olive is oval shaped and contains a seed. Usually, unripe olives are green while ripe olives are purple-black. Olives ripen in the Hebrew month of Ab (the eleventh month of the Hebrew calendar) which corresponds to July–August on the western calendar. Ancient peoples used long sticks to shake olive tree branches with the result that ripe olives fell to the ground. Ripe olives were gathered and those allocated for oil were put into an olive press. Ancient olive presses were heavy hewed stones with a vertical stone wheel. The wheel was rotated by an animal (donkey or ox) or by persons. The oil and watery liquid squeezed from the pulp was separated in settling vats. Water sank to the bottom while oil floated on the top. Oil was drained through a linen cloth to remove impurities. Lamps such as the bridesmaids used required large amounts of oil to keep them burning. Often oil had to be replenished as often as every fifteen minutes (Matthew 25:9, NIV).

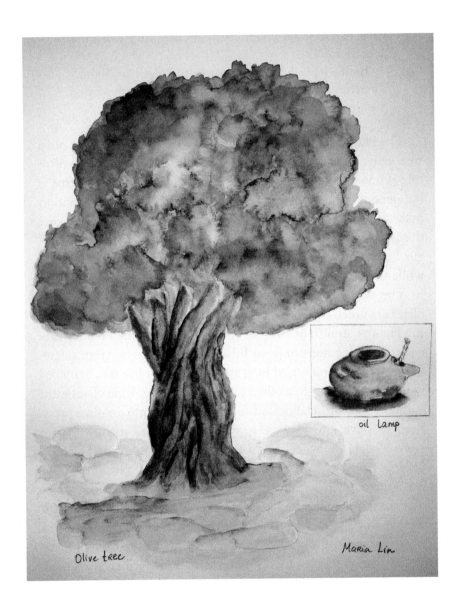

oil lamp

Olive tree

Maria Lin

Olive oil had a central place in Israelite history. In the Tabernacle, olive oil was the fuel for the seven Lamps on the Golden Candlestick. Olive oil was used to anoint and set apart kings, priest, and prophets. In ancient Palestine, olive oil was used for healing. The good Samaritan used olive oil to heal the wounds of the man who was robbed and beaten on his way to Jericho. In the early Christian church, olive oil symbolized the illuminating presence of the Holy Spirit. Through the Holy Spirit's presence, Christian actions shine in a dark world, healing the world.

The Holy Spirit illuminates or should illuminate a Christian's life to include his or her mind.

The Hebrew word for olive tree, olive, and olive oil was *zayith*, which means yielding illuminating oil.[1] Read, ponder, and discuss how the Holy Spirit illuminates or should illuminate your life. Some Bible verses that will aid you are:

a. John 14:16–18

b. John 16:8–13

c. Hebrews 10:16

The parable of the virgins with their lamps used imagery from wedding customs of first-century Palestine. The wedding feast took place in the evening; the day was filled with dancing and entertainment. At the day's end, the groom along with his good friends went to the home of the bride's parents. The bride left her parent's home and joined her groom. They headed to the groom's home to a banquet held in their honor. Friends joined the groom and bride along the way to their home. Often the procession was halted along the way for the couple to receive congratulations or share a toast. Eventually, the bride and groom reached the groom's home and enter it. The door was closed and the wedding feast began.

Some Bibles translate the ten virgins as "bridesmaids" who were typically girls younger than the bride. Perhaps, they were ten to eleven years old. If these girls were bridesmaids, for some reason they weren't a part of the groom and bride's procession. Rather, they waited at the groom's home. The bridal party was delayed; it didn't arrive until around midnight. The young bridesmaids fell asleep. The noise from the approaching bridal party woke them. Each trimmed her lamp—cut down the wick so the lamp wouldn't smoke. Five wise bridesmaids anticipated a delay in the bridal party's arrival. They brought an extra flask of oil to keep their lamps burning. The other five bridesmaids failed to bring extra oil.

In this parable the bridesmaids were central figures; however, their number isn't important. Just because the parable of the virgins identified an equal number of wise and foolish virgins doesn't mean that there will be an equal number of righteous and unrighteous individuals on earth at Jesus's second coming. Likely, Jesus gave the figure to round out the story.

In the Bible, the bridegroom is synonymous with Jesus, the Christ. Often the bride is the Christian church, composed of all who believe Jesus is the son of God and acknowledge him as Lord of their life (1 John 5:12). The interpretation of the parable of the virgins is that when Jesus comes the second time, it will be too late to rethink our lives or initiate a "do over" of life. At this time, Jesus's followers will enter into the wedding banquet with the bridegroom; they will have eternal life with God. The unprepared and foolish, who rejected or ignored Jesus, will be shut out. They will endure eternal punishment (Matthew 25:46).

The parable of the ten virgins wasn't about the son of God's first coming to earth; it is about his return to earth a second time. In the parable of the ten virgins, Jesus continued his assertion from Matthew 24 that only God knows when Jesus's second coming will occur. The parable is one of three, i.e., ten virgins, talents, and sheep and goats, with the same message. All emphasized the

GOD AS A GARDENER

truth that Jesus will come a second time and the importance of being spiritually prepared.

Both the Boy and Girl Scout mottos are "Be prepared."

1. The Scout motto means that scouts must be ready, willing, and able to do what is necessary in any situation that comes along, even in an emergency. Prepared means to plan in advance, make ready beforehand, and to work out the details. How could you use the Scout motto in your life as you wait for Jesus's second coming?

2. What do you have to plan so you will be ready for Jesus's second arrival? Alternatively, are you right where you should be and need no different preparation?

3. Probably, scouts prepare for an emergency by taking a cardiopulmonary resuscitation (CPR) class. List changes or actions you need to take to be optimally prepared for Jesus's second coming:

   a. _____

   b. _____

   c. _____

In first-century Palestine, only a minority of Jews still looked for the promised Messiah. Even fewer understood that Jesus, the Messiah, would come a second time. Generally, Jesus's disciples believed that his second coming would be soon after his ascension, even within their lifetimes. But, decades passed, decades turned into centuries, and centuries into millennia. For us living in the twenty-first century, it is easy to doubt that Jesus will come again. It's easy to fall asleep waiting for Jesus's second coming. It is easy to be unprepared, to stop planning ahead, so that if Jesus's return is delayed (by our standards of promptness), we are caught unaware and unprepared. When Jesus returns, individual preparedness will count. Preparedness can't be shared or transferred just as the wise virgins couldn't share their oil with the foolish ones.

Fearing and serving God and looking for the Messiah weren't futile. These activities had long-term rewards. Similarly, Christians living a life consistent with God's laws and statutes now will have long-term rewards.

Reference

1. Strong, James. *The New Strong's exhaustive concordance of the Bible.* Nashville, TN: Thomas Nelson Publishers, 2010.

Chapter 21

In-grafted Wild Olive Branch
Romans 11:16–24

Despite Jewish Christians starting the Christian Church in Rome, Gentile Christians resisted accepting Jewish Christians into their fellowship. Paul's letter to the Romans (about 71 AD) included a parable using cultivated olive and wild olive trees to illustrate Gentile's proper response to their Jewish Christian brethren.

Initially, the church in Rome was composed of Jews who believed that Jesus was the Messiah. The Church in Rome wasn't started by an apostle, but by Jews who returned from Pentecost in Jerusalem (Acts 2). Almost immediately, Jewish believers evangelized Gentiles. Then, Emperor Claudius banished all Jews from Rome. For twelve years, the Christian church in Rome consisted of only Gentiles. When Nero became emperor, he invited the Jews back to Rome, noting that they were good for business and trade. The problem was that Gentiles refused to allow Jewish Christians back into the Christian church in Rome. Perhaps Gentile Christians concluded that Emperor Claudius's rejection of the Jewish Christians meant that God also rejected them. Because Rome was the capital city of the Roman Empire, this discriminatory attitude had the potential to spread beyond Rome.

Put yourself in the role of a Jewish Christian who started the church in Rome.

1. How would you feel about this church—this body of believers in Rome? Would you be emotionally tied to them? Feel you have a vested interest in the church?

2. Ponder your feelings when you returned to your home church in Rome after twelve years of forced exile only to find that members didn't welcome when you returned. Identify, record, and verbalize how you as a Jewish Christian would have felt.

Paul focused his evangelistic efforts on the Gentiles—that is, individuals who weren't Jews. He named himself the apostle to the Gentiles. Paul spent years journeying throughout the Roman Empire converting Gentiles and strengthening their commitment to Jesus as Christ (the Messiah, the son of God). In Paul's letter to the church in Rome, Paul made it clear that the current parable was designed for Gentile believers (Romans 11:13). He wrote it to counter Roman Gentile's arrogant belief that they were better than Jewish Christians. One basis for Gentile arrogance was that unlike Jews, Gentiles didn't reject Jesus and lobby for his crucifixion. Further, the Gentile converts never denied that Christ rose from the dead as many Jerusalem Jewish leaders denied the resurrection. Here is the parable of grafting wild olive branches onto a cultivated olive root that Paul wrote to the Romans:

> If the root is holy, so are the branches. If some of the branches have been broken off, and you, though a wild olive shoot, have been grafted in among the others and now share in the nourishing sap from the olive root, do not boast over those branches. If you do, consider this: You do not support the root, but the root supports you.
>
> You will say then, "Branches were broken off so that I could be grafted in."
>
> Granted. But they were broken off because of unbelief, and you stand by faith. Do not be arrogant, but be afraid. For if God did not spare the natural branches, he will not spare you either.
>
> Consider therefore the kindness and sternness of God: sternness to those who fell, but kindness to you, provided

that you continue in his kindness. Otherwise, you also will be cut off. And if they do not persist in unbelief, they will be grafted in, for God is able to graft them in again. After all, if you were cut out of an olive tree that is wild by nature, and contrary to nature were grafted into a cultivated olive tree, how much more readily will these, the natural branches, be grafted into their own olive tree! (Romans 11:16–24, NIV)

In the parable of the in-grafted wild olive branch, Paul identified a) a root and branches (boughs) of a cultivated olive tree, b) a branch (bough) of a wild olive tree, and c) grafting a wild olive branch onto a cultivated olive tree. The original cultivated olive tree with its root and branches is the promises God made to Abraham, Isaac, Jacob, and their offspring, the Jews. This root was solid and sure. Jews who believed in Jesus as Messiah were the original root and branches of the early Christian church. Branches broken off from the cultivated olive tree were Jews who refused to believe that Jesus was the long-looked-for Messiah. This was the majority of Jews who lived in Palestine and throughout the Roman Empire at the time. The wild olive branch equated to Gentile Christians who believed that Jesus was the son of God and followed his teachings. The interpretation of Paul's parable in the eleventh chapter of Romans is that the Gentile believers were grafted into—became an integral, productive offshoot—of the Jewish faith.

Put yourself in the role of a Gentile Christian who was a member of the church in Rome.

1. Would you have been secretly glad to see the Jewish Christians leave town? After all, now the group would be more homogenous, all would be Gentiles.

2. When the Jewish Christians returned to Rome and wanted to again fellowship in the Christian church, what would have been your response—anger, disdain, resent-

ment, even fear that the returning Jews would try to take over the church?

3. How would Paul's parable in Romans 11 make you feel more or less secure?

Although Paul's parable seems easy to interpret, it has nuances that are only made clear by understanding characteristics of both cultivated and wild olive trees and the grafting process in olive trees. Paul identified that a wild olive branch was grafted onto the root of the cultivated olive tree; however, olive growers rarely graft wild olive branches onto cultivated olive trees. In reality, just the opposite occurs: growers graft cultivated olive tree branches onto wild olive tree roots. Paul was aware of this normal grafting procedure; he wrote that his parable was contrary to nature (Romans 11:24). Perhaps, Paul believed that making his point was more important than technical accuracy about olive tree grafting.

Horticulturists identify three reasons for tree grafting: 1) to propagate trees that don't root well by cutting a shoot from the poorly growing tree and grafting it onto a healthy tree, 2) to obtain a stronger root system, and 3) to grow plants faster. Importantly, the root sustains the newly grafted branch; the newly grafted branch doesn't sustain the root.

In Paul's parable, all three reasons support grafting the newly converted Gentile believers into the roots of Judaism. Gentiles used the structures and traditions of the established Jewish faith as roots for their worship of Jesus. An example is the Jewish tradition of meeting weekly to read, hear, and study God's word. Using this Jewish tradition, new Christian church members fellowshipped regularly and became more knowledgeable about their faith. Further, the Jews had sacred God-inspired writings. Knowing about and hearing Jewish scriptures (Old Testament) facilitated more ready acceptance of the New Testament gospel and letters. In these ways, the Christian faith grew stronger and faster, and became a deeper part of Gentile convert's lives. The new Gentile believers and churches acquired spiritual richness and fertility by being grafted into the deeply rooted, cultivated olive tree.

Although the cultivated olive tree formed the root and some branches of the olive tree in Paul's parable, the in-grafted wild olive tree branch resonates with most of us. We are the wild olive branch. Today, Gentile believers form most of the body of believers in churches in westernized countries.

Common names for the wild olive tree are oleaster and Russian olive.[1] Wild olive trees are often twelve to fifteen feet tall, so they are more often a shrub than tree. Wild olive trees are multitrunked and often grow as wide as tall. Wild olive trees grow almost everywhere, e.g., brackish water and river bottoms where water level is seldom more than two feet below ground surface. They are drought-tolerant and indifferent to wind and heat. The spreading growth pattern and diversity of growth sites of wild olive trees mirrored the growth of the new Christian church. Gentiles (non-Jewish) were almost everywhere in the Roman Empire. The Christian church appeared and thrived even in the most inhospitable environments.

The wild olive tree has a deep taproot (central root) and well-developed lateral roots. As it looks for water, the wild olive tree sinks its main root deep into the soil, while spreading horizontally in search of nutrients. This diverse root system adds to the stability of the wild olive tree. About 80 percent of the United States population self identifies as Christians. Like the wild olive tree, many have a root deep in their Christian faith. At the same time, they aren't necessarily tied to one religious denomination. They spread horizontal roots in search of an optimal church family.

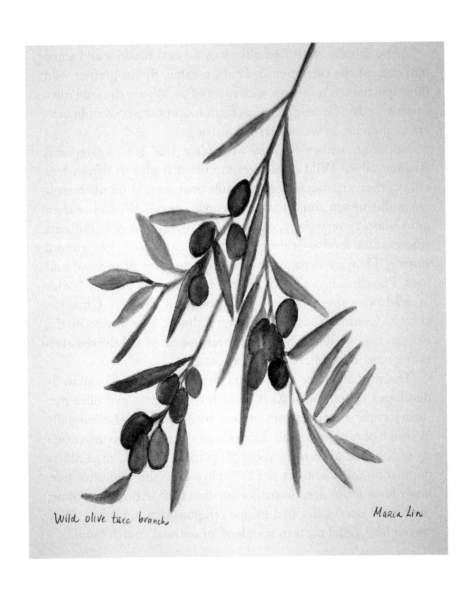

Wild olive tree branch   Maria Lin

Like the cultivated olive tree, the wild olive produces a drupe-like fruit; however, fruit is smaller than and not as tasty as olives from cultivated olive trees. In most countries, wild olives aren't eaten. Generally, the fruit isn't used to make olive oil. In Paul's parable, a wild olive branch was grafted onto a cultivated olive tree; however, the wild olive branch would never produce the same olive that grows on a cultivated olive tree. Similarly, Christianity is a unique religion and doesn't produce the same fruit as Judaism.

In your church do you have tiers or levels of individuals, i.e., some who are more important than others?

Using Paul's carefully written words in the entire eleventh chapter of Romans and particularly the parable of the in-grafted wild olive branch, answer the following questions.

1. What groups are more important than other groups in your church?

2. What groups are you in? Describe, discuss, and explain your conclusions. As you write or verbalize your answer, forget about a "socially acceptable" response, or even a "Christian" response. Write/verbalize your true feelings.

3. What do you think Paul would conclude about your church from your answers?

Despite the seeming lesser value of wild olive tree products than cultivated olive tree products, Paul's parable didn't mean that Jewish Christians were more valuable than Gentile Christians. Similarly, although Jewish Christians were represented by branches (more than one) and Gentile Christians by a single branch didn't mean that there were more Jews than Gentiles in the Christian church at Rome. Probably the opposite was true. Data aren't available for the number of Jews who became believers in the early centuries after Christ's death, but by the early twenty-first century, the vast majority of Christians are Gentiles. Globally, less than one-half percent of Jews self identify as Messianic Jews—that is, Jews who believe in Jesus as Messiah.

Paul's purpose in writing the parable of the in-grafted wild olive branch was to remind Gentile believers that the root of the Christian faith was in God's covenants with the Jews, i.e., God promised to bless all nations through Abraham's seed. When Paul reminded the Rome church about God's promise, he wanted to encourage a fully integrated church. Paul wasn't attempting to make the Christian church in Rome a sect of Judaism, nor was he advocating that Gentile Christians replaced the Jews in God's favor.

Is Christianity an inclusive or exclusive faith?

Reference

1. Dirr, Michael A. *Manual of woody landscape plants.* Champaign, IL: Stipes Publishing LLC, 2009.

Chapter 22

Productive versus Thorn-Infested Land

Hebrews 6:7–8

The Hebrews' author inserted a short two-verse parable to aid reader's intuitive understanding of a more difficult Christian truth (Hebrews 6:4–6). He believed that an agricultural parable about land producing crops versus thorns and thistles was an illustration that even the most urban reader of the first century could understand. Hebrews was addressed to Jewish Christians, but was relevant to Gentile Christians as well. For centuries biblical scholars believed that Paul wrote the letter to the Hebrews. Within the past five hundred years other writers, i.e., Barnabas and Apollos, have been proposed. Who wrote Hebrews is not as important as its message.

Immediately prior to the parable of productive versus nonproductive land, the writer reprimands readers because they were slow to learn (Hebrews 5:11–14). He wants them to become more mature in their faith, moving beyond learning or relearning elementary teachings about Jesus and Christianity to more mature doctrine (Hebrews 6:1–2).

What do you expect a bean plant to produce?
What do you expect a fig tree to produce?
What do you expect a thorn tree to produce?

Read Matthew 7:15-20, then answer the following questions:

1. How can you differentiate between a good tree and a bad tree? What about a good and bad person?

2. Can thornbushes produce grapes and fruit? How do bad people produce good fruit?

3. What will God do to a tree that doesn't produce good fruit? What should a Christian do to a purported Christian that doesn't produce good fruit?

In Hebrews 6:4–6 are statements that include some of the most hotly contested beliefs among Christian scholars, not to mention among Christian denominations. The writer asked: can an individual who has rejected Christ, after he has been enlightened and shared in the blessings of the Holy Spirit, be brought back to repentance? The writer averred that these believers—who have fallen away—crucify Jesus all over again and subject Jesus to public disgrace. Then, the writer provided a parable to illustrate his point:

> Land that drinks in the rain often falling on it and that produces a crop useful to those for whom it is farmed receives the blessing of God. But land that produces thorns and thistles is worthless and is in danger of being cursed. In the end it will be burned. (Hebrews 6:7–8, NIV)

Notice that the subject of the parable is the land—not rain, not a farming process, not a crop, not a farmer, but land. The land receives rain and does something with the rain. In one instance the land responds by producing a useful crop. In other words, the land produced grains, trees, herbs, etc., that gave the farmer food for his family. Possibly, the crop was abundant enough so that some food could be sold thereby enhancing food security for an entire community. In contrast, other land responds to the rain by producing thorns and thistles. This land is worthless to the farmer. It is in danger of being cursed; in the end it will be burned.

When my parents planted our garden in the 1960s, they first turned over the soil with a gas-operated, two-handled rototiller. Then, neat, straight rows (Dad was vehement that they be straight) were scored for seeds. After children hand dropped seeds, Dad and Mom covered the seeds using a hoe.

Jesus's parable of the sower and seed could have been the impulse for the Hebrews' parable (Matthew 13:3–23). In Jesus's parable, the farmer broadcast his seed. My Dad and Mom would have been horrified at the waste of good seed! Notice what happened to the broadcast seed; pay particular attention to the seed that fell among thorns.

1. Some seed fell on the pathways. On pathways the soil was packed down by people who walked on the path. Some pathway seed was eaten by birds. The analogy is to a person who hears the good news about Christ, but shrugs it off. What Jesus did for him or her doesn't penetrate into their head or heart. Governor Felix in Acts chapter 24 is an example of seeds that fell along the pathway. Despite hearing Paul preach several times, Felix wouldn't commit to Christ.

2. Some seed fell on thin soil. When soil is thin, it can't support the plant's root structure or retain water. Soon after, the plant rises through top soil the sun's scorching heat kills it. Some individuals who hear the gospel get all excited and decide they believe it. They may even make a profession of faith for Christ; but because their commitment is superficial, almost immediately they return to their old beliefs, old ways of thinking, and old ways of behaving. The sorcerer Simon reflects seed that fell on thin soil (Acts 8:9–25). Likely Simon was even baptized; however, his attempt to purchase the power to lay hands on converts so he could impute the Holy Spirit to them, demonstrated an almost immediate return to his old ways of thinking.

3. Some seeds fell among thorns. In this example persons hear the good news of Christ and accept it. Outwardly,

they say and do things that imply they have embraced a life for Christ. Often we encounter them in church. But life challenges and possibly the deceitfulness of wealth choke their newfound belief in Christ. Sometimes they stop attending church. Even when they continue to attend church, their life doesn't produce fruit for Christ. Ananias and Sapphira are an example of seed that fell among thorns (Acts 5:1–11). This husband and wife were Christian converts in the early Jerusalem church. Both were swayed by desire for admiration and prestige to lie to church leaders about the amount of money they were paid for a field they sold.

4. Some seed fell on good soil and this soil was deep enough for the plant to develop a good root structure and retain water for the plant to grow. If and when thorns sprung up around this good plant, it was rooted deep enough that it didn't succumb to the thorns and cares of the world. It produced a crop for Christ. Not all plants produced the same amount of crop. Some produced thirty, some produced sixty, and others produced a hundred times what was sown, but all yielded a crop. Early church leaders such as Paul, Titus, Priscilla, and Aquila are Bible examples of seed that fell on good soil.

According to the Hebrew's writer, land that produces thorns and thistles is worthless and in danger of being cursed. Think more deeply about Ananias and Sapphira. They made a public profession of faith in Christ. They were baptized. Probably, both had the Holy Spirit imputed to them either at Pentecost or by apostles laying hands on them. Apparently, they were part of the Jerusalem group that believed Christ was Messiah. Yet, Satan filled both of their hearts with the fear that if they gave the entire value of the sold field, they wouldn't have sufficient money. Both died unrepentant. When they lied about the payment for the field they sold, they crucified Christ all over again and certainly subjected Christ to public disgrace.

What is the effect of rain or fertilizer on a thorn-infested field?

1. Will increasing the amount of rain that falls on the thorn-infested land cause the land to produce good crops? What will happen when the thorn-infested land receives more rain?

2. What happens to thorn-infested land when a farmer adds fertilizer to the soil? Will fertilizer on the thorn-infected land cause good crops to grow there?

3. What should a farmer do with a thorn-filled field?

Thorns were first mentioned in Genesis as a way God cursed the ground when he expelled Adam and Eve from Eden. Thorns grew on the acacia tree in the Sinai desert and on Jotham's thorn tree in the Promised Land. Isaiah warned Ahaz that the land around Jerusalem would become thorn infested because of his disobedience. In the Sermon on the Mount, Jesus asked if people can pick grapes from thornbushes.

The Mediterranean buckthorn is a slow-growing thornbush common in the Mediterranean Basin where Jewish converts lived in the first-century Christian church. The buckthorn is an unattractive shrub that doesn't normally grow in cultivated gardens or fields. It prefers to grow in poor soil that is gritty and highly eroded. Along with the thistle, the buckthorn is the last species to disappear when livestock overgrazed an area. I wonder if the Hebrews writer is telling us that individuals like Ananias and Sapphira often continue to attend church and fellowship despite their secret rejection of Christian beliefs?

Buckthorn branches

Buckthorn shrub

Maria Lin

Most gardeners and farmers don't view the Mediterranean buckthorn as attractive or desirable. Buckthorn is tangled and has many branches. Grayish stems are topped with thorny spikes. Small flowers are yellowish and inconspicuous. Initially green, fruit turns black when mature. Although birds like the fruit, humans find it bitter. The buckthorn fruit is an emetic and laxative; in large quantities it is toxic to humans. Certainly, Christians don't want to consume buckthorn fruit.

Aphids are attracted to the Mediterranean buckthorn. If the buckthorn grows in a damp climate, it tends to develop a fungal disease. Once aphids and fungus appear on plants, they often spread to more valuable plants in the area. Similarly, church-attending, seemingly Christian individuals with negative thoughts or wrong doctrine can spread their beliefs to others in the community of believers. Like the Mediterranean buckthorn, they have no value. The parable suggests that thorn-infested land should be burned as a strategy to remove it. Church leaders need to ponder the optimal way to remove buckthorn from their congregations; they can't allow false doctrine to continue in their community.

The Hebrew word for thorn (Isaiah 7:23–25) is *shayith* which translates as scrub, thorn, or trash.[1] Trash is debris from plant materials, something worth little or nothing. Trash is an excellent symbol for men and women who learned what Christ did for them, tasted the heavenly gift and goodness of the word of God, shared in the Holy Spirit, and then turned away from the goodness of God. The outcome for these individuals isn't the storehouse of God, but a burning trash heap.

The Hebrew word for thorn is *shayith*, meaning trash.

1. What would it take for the fallen-away individual to reestablish a relationship with Christ?

2. What is the likelihood that a person will reestablish a relationship with Christ after falling away?

3. If you have a loved one who falls away from belief in Christ, what can, or should, you do to try to restore them to Christ?

We aren't in Ananias and Sapphira's minds; consequently, we don't know if they were truly converted to Christianity. Acts gives the impression that they completed the Christian "to do" list, e.g., profession of faith in Christ as savior, public baptism, indwelling of the Holy Spirit, taking communion (body and blood of Christ), church attendance; but perhaps, they didn't have a personal, relationship with Christ. Alternatively, perhaps this early church couple moved deliberately away from Christ. Worldly events became more attractive than Christ. Whatever happened in this couple's life, we don't want the same thing to happen to us. We don't want to crucify Christ anew or subject him to public disgrace. We don't want to die unrepentant.

Do you know anyone who was a believer, then rejected Jesus? Then returned to Jesus a second time? How is their witness for Jesus viewed by non-Christians?

Reference

1. Strong, James. *The New Strong's exhaustive concordance of the Bible.* Nashville, TN: Thomas Nelson Publishers, 2010.

Chapter 23

Grass in the Field
1 Peter 1:23–26

In Jesus's Sermon on the Mount, he included the parable of lilies adorning grass. In contrast to Jesus's emphasis on flowers, Peter's parable mentioned flowers, but focused on field grass. Peter encourages Christians to live a holy life because their physical life on earth is short and then comes a great reward. Belief and hope in Jesus means eternal spiritual life with him. In his letter, Peter quoted almost verbatim from a parable given initially by the prophet Isaiah. Here is what Peter wrote:

> All men are like grass, and all their glory is like the flowers of the field; the grass withers and the flowers fall, but the word of the Lord stands forever. (1 Peter 1:24, NIV)

Most scholars agree that Silas acted as Peter's secretary and carried this letter to Christians in what is now inland Turkey. In his first letter, Peter draws comparisons between the transience of field grass and the brevity of mankind's life. The transiency of life is a common theme in the Bible. Both King David and Isaiah compared man to grass which soon withers and dies away (Psalm 37:2, Psalm 103:15, Isaiah 40:6). This year, the Roanoke Valley received an overabundance of rain; it is December and grass is still green. Yet, I remember when I lived in San Francisco. Sometimes, I drove over the Golden Gate Bridge and traveled up Highway 80 into the Sacramento Valley. June through August, and even into September and October, the grass along the highway was brown and appeared dead.

Some of my days go fast. Others seem to drag!

1. Why do so many Bible writers describe life as short? Short in comparison to what? Does each of your days seem short? Why or why not?

2. Did you learn in school Edna St. Vincent Millay's words: "My candle burns at both ends; it will not last the night; but ah, my foes, and oh, my friends—it gives a lovely light!"[1] How do you think this small poem relates to physical life?

3. Look up the definition of an annual and a perennial plant? Which type of plant do you most identify with? If you had a choice of being an annual or a perennial plant, which would you chose?

In Israel, there were scores of grasses in the local flora. One of the most valuable native grass species was known as orchard grass. Orchard grass grew wild on hillsides and in shallow areas, in both sun and shade. Most likely orchard grass covered the large slopes where crowds sat to listen to Jesus's sermons and smaller areas where Jesus took Peter and other disciples for private talks. In Israel, rain falls October through March. In those months, grass is green and carpets hills. As spring progress into summer, grass turns brown from the scorching heat of the sun and lack of rain. Grass and wildflowers dry and turns into brown straw.

Orchard grass is a perennial plant. That means that even though it dies in the summer, grass regrows the following year. Orchard grass produces a flower head called a panicle. Seeds are produced in the flower heads. Initially, seeds are green but turn brown as they mature, then seeds drop to the ground. Although some seeds are carried away by the wind and others eaten by birds, most remain where they drop. Seeds enter the soil, germinate when it rains, and regrow the following year.

Grass of the field   Maria Lin

Peter told the Christians that they were born again with imperishable seed—the word of God (1 Peter 1:23). In the Bible, the Word of God is the living Christ. The apostle John wrote that in the beginning was the Word and the Word was with God and the Word was God (John 1:1). Christians are born again by believing that Jesus is God's son and savior of the world. In his physical body, Jesus died on the cross. Most living men and women will die unless Jesus returns to earth first. After physical death, Jesus rose from the dead. The interpretation of this parable is that individuals who believe in Jesus and who die physically will rise again. Why—because they are born again with the imperishable seed of belief in the Word of God (1 Peter 1:23).

As a Christian, you are born with imperishable seed!

1. How are Christian men and women perishable?

2. How are Christian men and women imperishable?

3. Differentiate between the physical you and the spiritual you.

King David, Isaiah, Peter, and Jesus made the point that life is transient by comparing man's life with field grass. They were all correct that grass withers and dies, and that physical life is transient, it withers and dies. At the same time, most field grass is a perennial. It withers and dies with the heat of the sun and lack of rain. Most field grass has a deep root structure and it produces seeds which germinate and grow the following season.

Individuals who don't believe that Jesus is the son of God die like field grass at the end of a season. In contrast, we, who are born by the Word of God, are perennials. Our root structure is firmly embedded in Jesus. We produce seeds of righteousness. Even if our physical bodies wither and die, the spiritual part of us will live with Jesus in heaven. As Peter wrote, we are born again not of perishable seed but of imperishable seed (1 Peter 1:23).

How do we get to be born again so that we never perish?

1. If you aren't sure, read, ponder and explain:

    a. Romans 3:22–23

    b. John 3:16

    c. 1 John 5:11–12

2. Do you need or want to take any action as a result of reading these verses, or are you where you want to be?

The New Testament Greek word for grass is *chŏrtŏs* which comes from a word meaning a pasture.[2] Pastures had important meaning to the ancient Israelites. Jeremiah (50:7) wrote that God was the true pasture of the Israelites. King David declared that the Lord is our shepherd and makes us lie down in green pastures (Psalm 23:2). Jesus named himself the good shepherd (John 10:9–14). Sheep only lie down in pastures when they feel secure. When sheep feel threatened, they stand up and look around seeking the source of peril. God's sheep never need to feel threatened. With Jesus as our shepherd, we can rest contentedly in green meadows. We don't have to fear life in this world or the next.

> **Remember when individuals described a good life as being in "deep cotton?" How is that similar, or different, from lying down in green pastures? Spiritually, are you living in "deep cotton?"**

References

1. Millay, Edna St. Vincent. *First fig. A few figs from thistles.* New York, NY: Harper & Brothers, 1922.

2. Strong, James. *The New Strong's exhaustive concordance of the Bible.* Nashville, TN: Thomas Nelson Publishers, 2010.

Chapter 24

Wormwood, a Shooting Star
Revelation 8:10–11

John the Apostle is the writer of Revelation. He recorded a vision that involved angels, one after the other, blowing trumpets. With the sounding of each trumpet, something occurred on earth. When an angel sounded the third trumpet, a star, blazing like a torch, fell to Earth. The name of the blazing star was Wormwood. In the Bible wormwood is a plant, more specifically a bitter herb.

When the first trumpet was sounded, a mixture of hail, fire, and blood was hurled down onto the earth. The result was a major ecological catastrophe; one-third of trees and one-third of green grass were burned up. When an angel sounded the second trumpet, something like a huge blazing mountain was thrown into the sea. The result was that one-third of sea creatures died and one-third of ships were destroyed. The result of both trumpets unleashed devastation on the world; however, the sounding of the third trumpet was significant in that for the first time John recorded that people died from the effect of the trumpet sounding. Wormwood, the falling star, caused one-third of earth's fresh waters to turn bitter. Many people died from drinking the bitter waters.

Customarily, bitterness is harmful or destructive to our soul, which is composed of our mind, emotions, and will.

1. Your will encompasses your disposition, inclinations, passions, appetite, even your desires. It is how you normally act. How can your will be influenced by bitterness and poisoned by how you live your life?

2. If you don't like or want some of your desires, what strategies can you implement to remove them from your life?

    a. _____

    b. _____

    c. _____

3. Identify at least one strategy that you will start implementing today.

Perhaps twenty-first century, more than first-century, readers can relate to John's vision of a star falling to earth and contaminating one-third of the earth's fresh water. We understand that the planet Earth isn't alone in the cosmos. Celestial events have, do, and will impact our planet and lives. When we read about a star falling to earth, we think of a meteorite (children call them shooting stars) or a comet that enters earth's atmosphere and lands on the earth. Because the celestial traveler doesn't burn up as it passes through the earth's atmosphere, the falling star will be large.

Moving from a falling meteorite or comet to bitter water requires deductive thought. Perhaps the cosmic traveler contained contaminated particles released as it moved through the earth's atmosphere. When those contaminated particles fall to the earth, they poison fresh water. An alternative explanation is that when the meteorite lands on the earth's surface, it sends dust into the air. If the earth's surface contains high levels of pollutants, these pollutants rise into the atmosphere. With the rotation of the earth and wind patterns, polluted particles spread around the globe. When these contaminants fall back to the earth's surface, they contaminate rivers, lakes, streams, and other fresh water used for drinking.

The recipients of John's letter understood the significance of one-third of the fresh water turning bitter. Mankind needs fresh water to live. Although a person can live around twenty-one days without food, few can live more than three to five days without water when the temperature is about 70 degrees Fahrenheit. In tropical areas where temperatures are substantially higher or in extremely dry climates like in the Middle East, individuals survive less time without fresh water. Thirsty people will do one of two things: die from dehydration or drink the contaminated water and die from its poison.

Currently, a United States city has a contaminated water supply. Despite the water's appearance, city officials assured residents that the water was drinkable. Adults drank it, cooked with it, and gave it to their children to drink.

Bitter water wasn't a new idea to early Christian Jews, even Gentile Christians. Most knew every step of the Israelites exodus from Egypt. They remembered that three days after the Israelites left Egypt they arrived at the spring at Marah in the Desert of Shur. At Marah, the Israelites expected to find fresh water; instead the water was bitter and undrinkable. The Bible didn't identify what made the Marah spring water undrinkable; however, Moses's action provided a clue. God told Moses to throw a piece of wood into the spring. Jewish rabbis believe the wood was from a mangrove tree, one of the few trees that leaches saline from water.[1] The result was that the Marah spring water became drinkable. The reverse of the miracle at Marah happened in John's visual parable: instead of bitter water becoming sweet, sweet water became bitter. In Revelation, God's action of causing Wormwood to fall on earth was to get people's attention and cause repentance.

Wormwood   Maria Lin

Although the Hebrew word for wormwood (*laanah*) is used about eight times in the Old Testament, in the New Testament the name Wormwood is used only for this blazing star in Revelation.[2] In the Old Testament, wormwood is synonymous with a bitter taste or poison. It was used as a metaphor for Israel's idolatry, calamity and sorrow, and false judgments. In reality, wormwood is an herb, native to the eastern Mediterranean area to include Israel. With the exception of rue, wormwood was the bitterest herb known in ancient times. Wormwood is an appropriate name for a blazing star that contaminates fresh water and brings death to millions of the earth's people.

Similar to the bitter feelings which occur and reoccur after loved ones die, the plant wormwood recurs; as a perennial it regrows year after year. Ancient people believed that if wormwood was hung to dry, it couldn't be placed in full sun or its aromatic properties would be lost. In contrast to many plants that thrive in sunny locations, wormwood prefers to grow in the shade. In earlier centuries, a shade was a ghost, a disembodied spirit. Often shades appeared in dimly lit locations. The shade-loving properties of common wormwood echoed the pall and moral decay that was endemic in ancient Israel and Judah before the nations were conquered. Both nations worshiped idols and foreign gods.

Spiritually, John's visions depicted events near the end of the ages. The purpose of these calamities and judgments on earth was to cause mankind to repent. Imagine the effects of the first three judgments on the earth. One-third of trees and plants will be destroyed. Food will be scarce. Maritime trade will be curtailed with destruction of one-third of the earth's ships. Many luxury items from foreign countries will be unavailable, i.e., spices, technological items, fruits, and vegetables. Oil imported to heat homes, fuel vehicles, and support manufacturing will be reduced substantially. When we turn on a water faucet, water may be undrinkable. Family and neighbors will die. People will be sorrowful and bitter over loss of life and loss of their livelihood.

> **At the deepest level our spirit gives us meaning and
> purpose. Our spirit enables us to love one another,
> our self, and God. It's through our spirit that
> we have communion and fellowship with God.**[3]

1. Is there anything in your spiritual life that you don't think is ideal or that you want to improve?

2. What are some strategies that you could use to improve your spiritual life, to improve your spirit?

   a. _____

   b. _____

   c. _____

3. Identify at least one strategy you will start today—and follow through on— to enhance your spiritual life.

When the seven seals were opened and the trumpets sounded, millions of earth's people died. Think of the bitterness these deaths causes on individuals who lost loved ones. Despite the severity of God's judgments, mankind refused to repent of their sins and acknowledge God as sovereign. The Bible says that people continued to worship demons and idols (Revelation 9:20–21).

> **How does personal bitterness poison us, e.g.,
> our thoughts, words, and character?**

References

1. Rabinowitz, Louis I. *Torah and flora*. New York, NY: Sanhedrin Press, 1977.

2. Strong, James. *The New Strong's exhaustive concordance of the Bible*. Nashville, TN: Thomas Nelson Publishers, 2010.

3. "Faith and Health Connection." Faith and Health Connection. http://www.faithandhealthconnection.org/.

Epilogue

Interpreting Plant Parable
for Future Generations

As you read this book, you saw plants illustrated in parables in both the Old Testament and New Testaments. And you learned how characteristics of the plant made the point of the parable. I related to spiritual truths explained by plants. I was reared in rural Pennsylvania. We grew most of our own vegetables. Our home was surrounded by flowers and fruit trees such as apple, apricot, cherry, and mulberry.

It is difficult, almost impossible, to interpret a parable when you can't relate to its physical dimensions. Let me give you an example. In addition to plants God used other physical phenomena or experiences in Bible parables to describe what he was like and what he expected of us. Some of these parables included animals, particularly sheep. Because my family didn't raise animals, I couldn't interpret parables illustrated by animals. In my middle years, I am still gaining insights into parables that describe sheep and a good shepherd that cares for them. My lack of knowledge about sheep and shepherding impeded my knowledge of God as a caring father.

How are pastors, parents, and teachers going to understand plant-based parables? How will they interpret these parables and teach them to children and new Christian adults who have little knowledge about growing and harvesting plants? I guess it is possible to show a video or even assign an interactive computer program about plant growth; but, seriously, what pre-teen, teenager or even adult is going to take the time to view such a program when Game of Thrones is an alternative?

The question is how are we going to make the Bible, filled with parables illustrated by plants, relevant to future generations? I am not sure I have a total answer, but some suggestions are:

1. Pastors and teachers themselves need to understand how plants grow and their characteristics to interpret the parables. In the future few of these leaders will have first-hand experiences with plants so the will need to complete in-depth study on plant growth patterns and uses.

2. Pastors and teachers can explain – probably using pictures – how the plant in a particular parable grows, what it looks like, and its uses. Remember, most children are concrete thinkers as are many new Christians. They need visual aids to interpret plant parables that describe God's nature and how God wants us to live a Christian life.

3. Show, tell, and excite. For example, show pictures of vegetables, herbs, and grains in various stages of growth and demonstrate how to winnow wheat. Show a fig and olive tree, contrasting their ripe and unripe fruit, good and bad fruit.

4. Plant and grow Bible plants at church. At our church we have a Bible garden and signs that label each plant. The sign gives the plant name and at least one reference where the plant is found in the Bible. Not only do we give tours of the garden to our church members, we offer them free to members of other churches and the community. Every summer, I give garden tours to children's Sunday school classes. We identify plants in parables and apply their meaning to children's lives.

This book on parables illustrated by plants is a first step in demonstrating, clarifying, and applying these parables in the current generation and into future generations. Bible scholar and plant scientists must work together to develop curricula on plants in the parables for all age levels. The Biblical Botanical Garden Society-USA (www.bbgsusa.com) is an excellent resource on Bible plants.

climate

Appendix A

Growing Parable Plants

Introduction

The Appendix is written for the gardener or want-to-be gar-
dener in many of us. Clues to successfully growing both Old
Testament and New Testament parable plants are included. At
St. John Lutheran Church in Roanoke, Virginia, we have a Bible
garden comprised of small plots around the front of the church.
In 2015, the church was awarded the Biblical Botanical Garden
Society-USA (www.BBGSUSA.com) Garden of the Year award.
Much of the information on growing Bible plants reflects trials
and error with growing Bible plants in our church garden.

The first pieces of information gardeners consider before buying a plant is whether or not it will not only survive, but thrive,
in the Plant Zone where they live. When Christians think of
the Holy Lands, for the most part they mean Israel, Syria, and
Jordan. In these countries, the climate is equivalent to United
States Plant Zone 8. That means even at night temperature don't
drop below 10 to 20 degrees Fahrenheit even in winter months.

Most Bible lands tend to be dry, with little precipitation
between late spring and mid-to-late October. Many Bible plants
are considered to be drought-tolerant, but that doesn't mean they
never need to be watered. I've included how and when to water
each parable plant. Often the produce, or fruit, of a tree or an
herbaceous plant was eaten by early people or their livestock. I've
included some of this information in this section.

Growing Old Testament Parable Plants

Aloe Trees

In many countries, aloe trees are on endangered tree lists. They are commonly called the eaglewood tree (*Aquilaria malaccensis* also known *Aquilaria agallocha*). Growing aloe trees is a challenge for home or church gardeners. Some optimism comes from India where many home gardeners now grow aloe trees to supplement family income. Arguably, northeast India produces the best aloe trees. Because aloe trees grow in the Philippines, I contacted a horticulturist in Hawaii to find out if they grow there. She responded that to her knowledge no aloe trees grow in Hawaii. Although aloe trees and aloes were mentioned several times in the Old Testament, aloe trees didn't grow in Israel, Syria, or Jordan. Currently, aloe trees aren't listed in Israeli plant databases.

The aloe tree is a tropical evergreen tree. Trees grow where summers are hot and average 93 degrees Fahrenheit in June and July. Winters are cooler at 50 degrees Fahrenheit in December and January. These average temperatures are higher than even the southern tip of Florida which means that gardeners in the United States, Canada, and Britain won't be able to grow the aloe tree.

In aloe tree-producing countries, overall annual rainfall varies between forty-seven to seventy-four inches. With rainfall at this level, humidity is high most of the year. Trees grow best in moist lowland tropics; however, aloe trees are found on sloping hills at elevations up to three thousand feet. The tree will grow in rocky as well as sandy loam soils.

Home and church gardeners will likely have little success trying to grow the aloe tree outside or even inside homes or churches. Aloe trees can grow in a greenhouse that mimics tropical conditions. Importantly, the aloe tree of the Old Testament is a different plant than the aloe (*Aloe vera*) of the New Testament.

Gardeners can plant the *aloe vera* and have an example of an aloe in their home or church garden.

Thorn Trees

Most arborists agree that Jotham's thornbush is the *Ziziphus spina-christi* called the jujube.[1] In Israel, the jujube bush grows around Samaria where Jotham lived. In the United States, nurseries sell it as *Ziziphus jujuba*. It is labeled as a tree, not a bush. Jujube trees are well adapted to Plant Zones 5 to 11. The tree is a deciduous evergreen. In most climates, leaves turn a bright yellow, then drop to the ground as external temperatures decrease. The jujube tree grows well in full sun, but will grow in lightly shaded areas.

Trees adapt to climates where rainfall is as low as four to twenty inches per year. Newly planted jujube trees grow best if watered weekly during hot months. Generally, mature jujube trees don't need to be watered; however, if a year is very dry, water monthly. Water heavily each time rather than more frequent shorter watering. In the deserts of southwestern United States, jujube trees are used in xeriscape gardens. The tree isn't particular about altitude and grows from sea level to 6,561 feet. Jujube trees prefer sandy soils and grow poorly in clay. Trees can grow in high saline and high alkaline soils; consequently, gardeners who live near seashores can safely plant them.

Few studies focused on fertilizer for the jujube. Probably, a general purpose annual fertilizer in the spring is sufficient. Surprisingly, unpruned trees produce as much fruit as pruned trees, but it is always good to remove damaged limbs. The tree develops a deep taproot. After being planted, it shouldn't be transplanted. Although jujube trees will grow from seeds, frequently, they are propagated from suckers that grow from tree roots or lower tree branches. Flowers contain both male and female organs so growers don't need two trees for fruit to develop.

Generally, jujube trees start to bear fruit three years after being planted. Most fruit resemble a large cherry. Immature fruit is green. As fruit ripens, it passes through a yellow-green stage with mahogany-colored spots on the skin. Mature fruit is red and soon begins to soften and wrinkle. Although wrinkled red fruit is eaten, many people prefer to eat the fruit in the interval between the yellow-green stage and the full red stage. At this time, fruit is crisp and sweet, reminiscent of a crab apple. Under dry conditions, jujube fruit loses moisture, shrivels, and become spongy inside. If picked when green, fruit will ripen off the stem.

We planted a *Ziziphus jujube* in our church Bible garden in Roanoke, Virginia. The Roanoke Valley is in Plant Zone 7. The tree is about two years old and about six feet tall. My husband planted the tree in early September and watered it weekly. Around the beginning of November, he mulched around it for overwinter protection. It is now April and buds are forming on the tree.

Spotted Golden Thistles

The spotted golden thistle's (*Scolymus maculatus*) origin is the Mediterranean Basin except on extreme seashores. It flourishes in very hot temperatures to include deserts. Spotted golden thistle tolerates cold. In the United States, gardeners can expect it to grow well in Plant Zones 6 to 9. The thistle appears in uncultivated lands and in abandoned fields and ditches. This thistle loves sun, but will grow in semi-shade and light woodlands.

Spotted golden thistle isn't particular about type of soil and can be found in sand, loam, and clay; however, soil must be well-drained. Although the spotted golden thistle grows in moist soil, it seems to wilt in a wet environment. You don't have to worry about irrigating thistle; it is drought-tolerant. I have never known spotted golden thistle to be fertilized to promote growth.

Just the opposite is true—United States gardeners wonder how to get rid of it.

Spotted golden thistle is an annual, erect plant that grows twelve to fifty-one inches tall in the United States. Its two outstanding features are its flower, which resembles the yellow dandelion flower, and its leaves. Actually, leaves are bracts rather than true leaves; they are tooth shaped (dentate) with a series of pointed margins. Notably, bract edges are outlined in white. Because edges are stiff and prickly, gardeners avoid them or wear gloves when gardening around them.

In late spring, fleshy parts of the spotted golden thistle leaves are harvested in Spain, Greece, and southern Italy. Although I have never eaten the leaves, some individuals describe them as a delicious vegetable which are used in soups, stews, and scrambled eggs. Leaves can be baked with cheese and used as a side vegetable with meat.

Spotted golden thistle is propagated from seeds produced in flowers which bloom in late spring or early summer. Seeds, known to germinate even after a long period of dormancy, are best planted in late winter. When seeds are intentionally planted, experts recommend application of an organic fertilizer.

Cedar Trees

Cedar trees *(Cedrus libani)* are native to the Middle East. The most venerable cedar representatives are 1,200 to 2,000 years old; they grow in northern Lebanon. In Lebanon, cedar trees are a protected species because so many have been harvested or destroyed. Lebanon cedars were introduced into the United States in colonial times.

Among the largest and most majestic trees, the Lebanon cedar grows to 100 to 120 feet with a main trunk diameter of six to eight feet. Generally, branches are densely packed. Lower branches sweep the ground. Cedars are evergreen with one-inch-long needles. In the United States, cedars of Lebanon grow in Plant Zones 5 to 7. The tree grows best in deep, well-drained loam soil, but overall growth rate is slow. Cedar trees can grow in rocky soil; roots extend deep into the ground. The Besharre mountainous region of northern Lebanon is about 2,000 to 2,500 feet above sea level.

Gardeners should plant cedars in an open, sunny area with plenty of space on all sides. The species doesn't tolerate shade or pollution. Reflecting its Middle East origins, Lebanon cedars grow best in a dryer atmosphere. For the most part, cedars don't need to be irrigated; however, newly planted cuttings need water if the season is exceptionally dry.

Native-grown cedars aren't fertilized or pruned; however, home gardeners may want to fertilize their trees annually to encourage them to grow more rapidly. A general-purpose fertilizer applied in spring after the last frost is best. Part of the beauty of a Lebanon cedar is its shape, so trees are generally not pruned. Young trees grow naturally in a pyramid shape.

Cedars begin to flower when about twenty-five to thirty years old. The flower is a cone. Both male and female cones grow on the same tree. Male cones are less than one-fourth inch thick and two inches long. Pollen is dispersed by the wind. Pollinated female cones take one to three years to mature. When mature, the female cone breaks apart and seeds are carried on winged scales. Seeds germinate best in the cool temperatures of high hills and mountains. The Lebanon cedar is the most difficult cedar tree to root from cuttings. Cedar tree cuttings form roots only about 30 percent of the time.[2]

In the United States, common names for so many trees include the word *cedar* but trees aren't true cedar trees, i.e., Atlantic white-cedar (*Chamaecyparis thyoides*), Northern white-cedar (*Thuja occidentalis*), and Easter red cedar (*Juniperus virginiaia*).[3] True cedars include the deodar cedar (*Cedrus deodara*) and atlas cedar

(*Cedrus atlantica*). The National Arboretum in Washington, DC, has a collection of Lebanon cedars.

Laurel Trees

The laurel tree (*Laurus nobilis*) is native to the Mediterranean Sea basin; consequently, it grows well where summers are long, hot, and tend to be more dry than wet. I have never seen them growing in deserts. Laurel trees tolerate both morning and afternoon sun. In extremely hot summer climates, light or dappled shade protects leaves and branches. The laurel tree is a good option for an understory tree such as below a large oak. Laurel trees won't grow near seacoasts, but do tolerate high winds. If your garden receives frost, plant laurel trees in a pot and take them inside during winter months. When you move a laurel tree for the winter, place it near a window facing south or east.

Laurel trees thrive in loam with leaf compost; be sure the soil is well-drained. Water newly planted laurel trees until they become well rooted. The rule is three-to-five gallons of water each week the first year the laurel tree is planted. After the first year, trees rarely need watering. Laurel trees are notorious for their slow growth, so don't be dismayed if your laurel tree doesn't grow several feet a year. Often laurel tree growth is measured in inches. Left unattended, laurel trees can form a small thicket; therefore, they are sometimes used as hedges. In spring when laurel trees experience what in a laurel tree is a growth spurt, they benefit from fertilizer. Commercial liquid tree fertilizer can be used or manure obtained from a local distributor.

In most United States plant zones, laurel trees loose leaves in winter and bloom anew in spring. After new growth has matured in the spring, laurel trees can be cut back and shaped. Foliage is thick. Leaves are a lustrous dark green, pointed, and feel leathery. Trees are easily to shape into a pyramid, cone, or globe and integrate well with various decors. Shaped laurel trees are often placed in church foyers or in the sanctuary.

Laurel trees can be grown from seeds or cuttings; however, purchasing a seedling from a nursery is the easiest way to get a laurel tree. Trees produce male and female flowers on separate trees; therefore, growers need both a male and female tree. Primarily, flowers are pollinated by bees. Ideally, laurel trees are planted and allowed to grow in place; trees won't thrive if moved repeatedly.

If you travel to Washington, DC, in the summer, the National Arboretum has several specimens of laurel trees that are shaped as globes and pyramids. These laurel trees are in pots; most likely they are kept inside in the winter. A few master gardeners including myself planted laurel trees here in the Roanoke Valley. Although smaller laurel trees tolerated several of our (Plant Zone 7) winters, all died within a few years. United States gardeners shouldn't substitute our beautiful Mountain Laurel (*Kalmia latifolia*) tree for the Bible laurel tree. These two trees are from different families and have different growth patterns.

Grapes

Most grapes are cultivars of the *Vitis vinifera* species. Concord, Niagara, and Catawba are native American grapevines. They are made into juice, jelly, and wine. Increasingly, grapes have been modified to grow in almost all climates; consequently, this entry focuses on optimal strategies for grape growth in a home or church garden, rather than for grape production on a large scale. Importantly, gardeners will want to investigate whether or not grapes will grow in their climate and which grape cultivars to plant. Overall grapes grow best in Plant Zones 5 to 7. To grow, flower, and set fruit, grapes need between 150 to 170 days with temperatures over 50 degrees Fahrenheit. Grapes grow best in full sun and do especially well when planted so they receive sun from the south.

Although grapes need a lot of water, moist, humid conditions aren't good for grape production. Once vines are established, they seldom need watering. The first year, water vines about once a week. Don't spray or mist. Overwatering causes leaves to drop. Grapevines are prone to both mildew and fungus; consequently, good air circulation is important. A windy area enhances air circulation around plants. Often grapes are planted on slopes. Warm air settles in pockets along slopes and in valleys, making these areas slightly warmer than surrounding areas. This microclimate variation has made the Great Lakes region of New York and other valleys in the United States and Europe ideal for grape production.

Grapes prefer rocky, sandy soil. They grow best where soil pH is slightly acidic (6.0 to 6.5), but can grow where pH is 5 to 7. Vine fertilization needs vary widely and makes valid recommendations difficult. A rule of thumb is that young vines don't need fertilizer for the first one to three years. When you apply fertilizer, do so in early spring only. Too much fertilizer cause winter damage of vines and delays grape coloring and ripening. Excess nitrogen causes grapevines to produce leaves and stems, but not flowers or grapes. When fertilizer is applied, gardeners should keep it about twelve inches away from the vine's base. Ideally, soil should be tested every three-to-five years to keep the pH acid. Mulching isn't necessary after vines are established.

Prune the vine when it is dormant, usually late winter, i.e., February, using a pruning tool that makes a clean cut on the vine. A clean cut puts less stress on the grapevine and creates less exposed surface for entrance of disease-causing organism. Year one pruning goal is to encourage vertical growth and prevent bushiness. Cut all lateral shoots that form on the vine. In the second year, you want to train two lateral shoots to climb the support structure. When the two main shoots have climbed as high as you desire, pinch off the ends to encourage tertiary shoots to fill out the available space. Trim off lower level lateral shoots.

Third year pruning and subsequent year pruning involves cutting one-year-old wood back to multinode fruiting spurs. Attempt to have spurs evenly spaced and pointed downward. A rule of thumb is to leave 80 to 90 percent of the previous year's wood and forty to fifty fruiting nodes each year. Remember, grapes only form on current year's growth.

Grape flowers have a delicate scent and each variety, merlot, Lombard, etc., have a different scent. Flowers turn into grapes. Only rarely do gardeners grow grape vines from seeds. Generally, vines are purchased from nursery stock. Gardeners can take cuttings from current well-established grapevines. Early-spring cuttings can be rooted directly in the soil. Grapevines can be propagated by layering.

Thorny Burnet

Thorny burnet plants (*Sarcopoterium spinosum*) grow in most Mediterranean Basin areas to include southern Europe, northern Africa, and the Middle East. Because it is salt resistant, thorny burnet plants grow along the Mediterranean Sea coast. In the United States, gardeners can plant thorny burnet along both seacoasts and the Gulf of Mexico. The thorny burnet tolerates light frosts, however, deep frosts and zero-degree temperatures similar to those in the northern United States damage plants. Despite general frost warnings, thorny burnet plants were found on lower slopes of Crete's White Mountains which reach eight thousand feet. If you live in a temperate climate and want to attempt to grow thorny burnet, consider planting them near your home or church wall to reduce the effect of cold temperatures.

Thorny burnet grows well in full sun even when temperatures reach 100 degrees Fahrenheit. Although the plant grows in many types of soil, it grows best in light gravel or red loam soil as long as soil is well-drained. Thorny burnet is listed as a drought-resistant plant so gardeners don't have to be concerned about watering them.

Plants grow wild and have little commercial value; consequently, growers have little interest in studying the effects of irrigation. Similarly, studies on the effect of fertilizer aren't readily available. While difficult to germinate, seeds are the most common method of propagating the thorny burnet plant. Vegetative propagation isn't reliable, i.e., use of cuttings and even layering.

Thorny burnet has been used on slopes and banks to control soil erosion. It can provide a protective habitat for birds and small mammals. Some gardeners identified thorny burnet as an excellent ground cover. When the thorny burnet is in bloom, orange-red buds are a cheerful addition to a garden. When I look at my pictures from The Biblical Landscape Reserve in Israel, I am attracted to the thorny burnet. Reddish flower buds appeared to be bursting forth everywhere on the bush. At times, native people used leaves as a pot herb, but only in times of severe famine.

Cumin

Cumin (*Cuminum cyminum*) is an annual herb that is the second most popular spice in the world. Cumin is a pungent flavor in European, Indian, and Mexican cuisine. Seeds from the plant date back four thousand years. In the United States, cumin grows in Plant Zones 5 to 10. When grown outside, plant cumin in full sun. If grown inside, place plants in front of a window that is sunny most of the day.

Cumin prefers a well-drained, fertile, sandy-loamy to loamy soil, but will tolerate diverse soil types. Cumin will grow in a pH range between 6.8 (mildly acidic) and 8.3 (alkaline); however, the ideal pH growth range is 7.0 to 7.5. After planting cumin seeds, water regularly, but don't overwater. Allow soil to go almost dry between watering then soak soil thoroughly.

Because cumin isn't frost hardy, often seeds are started indoors and transplanted outside two-to-four weeks after the last spring frost date. To increase germination rates, soak seeds in water for about eight hours before planting. Ideally cumin seeds are planted about one-fourth inch deep and four to six inches apart. If temperatures are warm, seeds will germinate in seven to fourteen days. Cumin plants grow anywhere from six to twenty-four inches tall. Cumin is ready for harvest in 100 to 150 days.

Ripe cumin pods become dry and turn brown. Harvest pods when the first ones are about to spill their seeds. After cutting the stem from the root, hang cumin plants upside down in a paper bag. The seeds will dry completely and fall to the bottom of the bag, or you can beat the bag to open seed pods. Sift the captured seeds, possibly outdoors when there is a gentle breeze, to remove the chaff. Place seeds in an air-tight container and store in a cool location out of direct sunlight.

Barley

Barley (*Hordeum vulgare*) is a grain that was domesticated in the Middle East between 7000 and 6000 BC. For Israelites, barley was a major food staple because it was less expensive to purchase than wheat. Barley grows best in full sun. Winter barley grows in cool ground. Ideal winter temperatures hover right around freezing; however, seeds tolerate lower, even zero degrees Fahrenheit winter temperatures. Winter barley is largely drought resistant and receives sufficient moisture through snow and rain.

Barley tolerates alkaline and saline soils. Soil should be well-drained sand or medium loam. Barley will grow at higher altitudes than wheat and can be planted on lower hillsides. Most farmers who grow barley as a cash crop fertilize soil before they plant seeds. An application of herbicide is sometime necessary to keep weeds out of large barley crops, even those growing in winter climates.

Growers in the United States reported that barley ripens in as few as forty to fifty-five days. In Israel winter barley was often planted for its early harvest date. Barley flowers (florets) are bisexual. Winter barley largely self pollinates. Barley passes through three growth stages. In the vegetative stage, seeds absorb water, swell, and roots develop; this stage occurs underground. The reproductive stage begins with the emergence of the first leaf from the soil. A leaf sheath grows which protects the embryonic barley plant. In the reproductive stage, the barley stalks, called spikes, grow to about thirty to thirty-five inches. Barley florets develop at the top of the spike. The final stage of barley growth occurs when grain fills the barley head (floret). Barley has six rows of kernels per spike. It is ready to harvest when it turns golden or cream in color and stalks are brittle. Because mature barley heads are prone to shattering with loss of grain, often barley is harvested just before it is fully matured.

Almond Trees

Almond trees (*Prunus dulcis*, also known as *Prunus amygdalus)* originated in the Middle East. They grow well in United States Department of Agriculture Plant Zones 5 to 9. They prefer full sun. Young almond trees are sensitive to drought for the first two years. If your area receives one inch of rain every ten days, supplemental water isn't needed. If rainfall is less, water trees with two-to-three gallons of water every ten-to-fourteen days. Add water slowly so it soaks into the soil rather than running off the top. Older tree are drought-tolerant and may not need supplementary watering.

Almond trees grow best in loamy soil that is well-drained. They don't tolerate waterlogged, drowning roots. A slightly alkaline soil pH (6.0 to 7.0) is ideal. Don't plant almond trees in soils that are heavy, such as clay soil. Plant almond trees when the ground isn't frozen. If a hard frost is expected, delay planting saplings until temperatures moderate. Plant a potted tree at the same depth as it was growing in the pot. Almond trees have one main root, called a taproot. Don't cut off or bend the taproot; curl it in the hole. Try to spread root hairs out (laterally) in the hole. Wet the root before planting and place two-to-four gallons of water in the tree's hole.

When you plant an almond tree, you can add manure, garden compost, or peat moss to top soil. Fertilize once per year—May is a good month—with compost, manure, or lime as needed. Often potted nut trees are pruned prior to being sold; however, assess your almond tree carefully. To get the tree off to a good start, cut it back so there is only one strong leader (sprout, stem). In subsequent years, prune when the tree is dormant; remove secondary limbs with narrow crouch angles and diseased or broken branches.

In 2005, self-pollinating almond trees were developed. If a self-pollinating variety is planted, only one tree is needed for almond production. Previously, it was necessary to plant both a female flowering tree and a male flowering tree for the female tree to produce almonds. Gardeners may still want to plant pollinating partners to increase the size of almond crops. Most trees begin to bear almonds in three to four years. Generally, almonds ripen from August through October.

Recently, arborists developed several dwarf varieties and semi-dwarf varieties of almond trees; some don't produce fruit. We planted a semidwarf tree in our church Bible garden; it is sterile but the flowers are beautiful. It is growing as a bush. Semidwarf almond trees grow to about fifteen feet tall while dwarfs top out at six to seven feet. Often almond tree trunks are painted with a white latex paint to prevent rodents from gnawing on the tree and to prevent sun scald.

Fig Trees

Figs were identified in written records as early as 9000 BC in Jordan. Trees grow best in warm, dry climates; probably fig trees (*Ficus carica*) are native to present-day Turkey, Iraq, and Iran. Many trees grow to about twenty feet tall. In the United States, often fig trees are smaller and many branches grow up from just above the ground. The plant looks more like a bush than a tree. Originally, fully dormant fig trees were hardy to 12-to-15 degrees Fahrenheit, while actively growing trees could be damaged by temperatures at 30 degrees Fahrenheit. Dormant buds were susceptible to frost. More recently, horticulturists developed hardy fig varieties. We have a "Brown Turkey" cultivar in our church garden that is exposed to winter nighttime temperatures of less than minus five degrees Fahrenheit. It has successfully weathered three winters and produces figs once a year.

The trunk of the fig tree is short; bark is sensitive to sun. In very hot climates, tree trunks are whitewashed to reflect sunrays. I'm not aware of fig trees that grow in the lower tier (Georgia through southern California) of the United States. Extremely hot sun, particularly in southwest deserts, inhibits their growth. The canopy of the fig tree can be as wide as the tree is tall. Fig tree roots spread far beyond the tree canopy in search of water.

Fig trees grow best in loam or sand. Soil must drain well. Trees survive better if set two-to-four inches deeper than grown in the nursery. Because most fig roots are close to the soil surface, they dry out easily. As soil dries, water fig trees. Slight leaf wilt is a sign that trees need water. Mulching aids moisture retention.

Generally, fig trees don't require regular fertilizer, and you shouldn't apply fertilizer when you plant a fig tree. Excess applications of nitrogen have a negative effect on fruit quality. The only exception is figs grown in containers. Containerized figs need to be fertilized about four times a year with a balanced tree fertilizer.

For a fig tree to grow as a tree rather than a multibranched bush, yearly pruning is necessary to remove all but the strongest vertical leader. Fig trees bear figs in the fall season. Prune the fig tree immediately after the main crop is harvested in the fall. Because figs bear fruit on the previous year's growth, heavy pruning results in lighter crops the following season.

After four years of growth, the fig tree begins to yield fruit. Ideally, figs are fully tree-ripened before they are picked. In Bible days, male and female flowers grew on separate trees. Tiny wasps (*Blastophaga psenes*) mature inside fig flowers and carry pollen from male to female flowers. Only flowers that are pollinated produce edible fruits. In 2005, self-pollinating fig trees were developed.

Broad Beans

The Bible bean was the broad bean (*Vicia faba*). Beans were one of the oldest cultivated plants, i.e., at least six thousand years. Their origin was North Africa or the Middle East. Broad beans grow best when temperatures are 60-to-65 degrees Fahrenheit. Where environmental temperatures are much over 80 degrees, bean production is decreased, quality lost, and pest problems abound. Beans grow well in northern United States and Canada where the optimal growing season is spring and summer. In these areas, gardeners plant seeds early in spring as soon as soil can be worked. Beans aren't frost sensitive and can tolerate temperatures down to about 15 degrees Fahrenheit. In southern United States and some Pacific coastal states, beans are a winter crop. They are planted around November and harvested in May. Beans won't tolerate maritime exposure.

Broad beans grow both in full sun and semi-shade (light woodland). The plant will grow in sand, loam, and clay soils. Soil pH can be acidic, neutral, or basic (alkaline). Broad beans don't require fertile soil. They manufacture their own fertilizer out of air by converting atmospheric nitrogen into a form of nitrogen that their roots can use. Beans like moist soil. Textbooks claim that broad beans are drought-tolerant, however, when temperatures are high, i.e., 90s, I water them using a soaker hose.

Broad beans can grow up to five feet tall. Bean plants are wind tolerant; however, because they grow so tall, heavy winds can blow them over. For this reason many gardeners use stakes to support their growth. Also, a good crop of beans makes plants top heavy; they may flop over if not staked vertically.

In the Roanoke Valley in western Virginia, we plant beans in early spring. Flowers appear May and June. They grow on short stems from the leaf axil and are white with a dark purple throat. Bean flowers are one of the most beautiful flowers in a garden. Flowers contain both male and female sex organs. Although bean flowers can self pollinate, many are pollinated by insects, particularly bees. Summer flowers transit into green bean pods. Each pod contains five-to-six broad beans which are flat on the sides. Harvest beans when beans can be seen on the outside and fill out the pods. Pods lower on a bean stalk mature before pods near the top. Pick low-growing beans first.

The broad bean flavor is mild and pleasant and can be cooked and eaten fresh. Broad beans can be dried and ground into flour. In ancient Israel, broad bean flour was made into bread and consumed by those living in, or near, poverty or in times of famine. Although not a source of complete protein, broad beans are a valuable protein source.

Cypress Trees

The Bible cypress tree (*Cupressus sempervirens*) is named both the common cypress and the Mediterranean cypress. As you would expect from its name, the cypress is native to southern Europe and northern Africa. Commonly, it grows in United States Plant Zones 7 to 9. Cypress trees are salt tolerant and can be planted near seashores. Trees are hardy to zero degrees Fahrenheit. Cultivars of the Mediterranean cypress are remarkably tall (up to 115 feet), but relatively narrow, rarely wider than eight feet. Trees are evergreen and leaves are needles.

Trees grow best in full sun; however, within this parameter, gardeners need to carefully select the landscape site when planting only one or two trees. Because of their great height and columnar shape, often cypress look best near the corner of a tall building to add a vertical accent. In most cases, a single tree in the middle of a garden or backyard looks out of place.

The Mediterranean cypress grows best in fertile soil, i.e., loam and sand, with good drainage. The tree grows well when started in containers and transplanted into soil. The first year after a tree is transplanted, water it weekly, particularly if rainfall is scarce. After they are established, cypress trees thrive in average to dry conditions.

Cypress trees grow rapidly when they are young (years one to three). Generally, they don't need fertilizer; however, they will benefit from application of a general-purpose fertilizer annually, preferably in the spring. The only times I have pruned a cypress is when a branch is damaged or when a branch grew out of shape and destroyed the silhouette of the tree.

On cypress trees, flowers are cones and one arborist noted that cones only develop in climates that have cool winters. Although trees produce both male and female cones, often they are dominant at different times. For example, male cones grow on older branches and on trees that are stressed. In contrast, female cones grow on younger trees and on extension-growth branches. The rate of extension growth on a cypress tree controls female cone production and reproduction. In nature, cones are wind pollinated. Most cypress trees grow from cuttings.

Note: The common bald cypress (*Taxodium distichum*) in southeastern United States is a different genus and species of tree than the Mediterranean cypress.

Myrtle Trees

The Bible myrtle (*Myrtus communis*) originated in the Mediterranean region and the Middle East, therefore, grows best where winters are cool and summers are long and hot. Trees tolerate maritime (salt) air. They are hardy to temperatures as low as five degrees Fahrenheit, but can be damaged by cold, dry wind and late frosts. Myrtle trees grow best in full sun and don't tolerate shade. In Israel, myrtle trees grow wild on the Golan Heights which are 3,300 feet high; consequently, in the United States, myrtle will grow in both flat lands and piedmont areas.

Myrtle trees are resistant to drought as you would expect in a tree native to the Middle East; however, they don't grow naturally in desert areas. They grow in most reasonably fertile soils as long as the soil is well-drained. If your area receives no rain for three to four weeks, water your myrtle trees. When adding water, use a full two to three gallons of water on each tree. Application of fall and late spring mulch is a good idea.

Cultivated myrtle trees will benefit from a general-purpose fertilizer each spring when new tree growth starts on trees. Ornamental myrtle trees are pruned to obtain a desired shape; however, pruning, other than to remove dying or broken limbs, isn't required or even optimal. Myrtle trees aren't meant to be shaped, but to grow naturally.

Myrtle can grow as a small tree; however, most myrtle plants grow as a shrub (less than sixteen-to-twenty feet tall). Dark green leaves contain oil-secreting glands and are fragrant. The myrtle tree produces one of the most beautiful flowers in nature. The white flower has five petals and numerous long stamens with yellow anthers. Myrtle trees are self fertile and are pollinated by bees which brush against anthers and carry polling into the ovary of the flower. In addition to growing plants from seeds, gardeners can get new myrtle trees from tree cuttings (from nonflowering tree shoots).

Most gardeners are unaware that the myrtle tree produces a purple-black berry called a *mursin*. When dried and ground, mursins are used to flavor stews and meats. The mursin can be boiled to produce a jelly and a beverage. In the United States, we rarely eat mursins and they are not sold in most general-purpose food stores.

The Bible calls the myrtle a "leafy tree" and traditionally the tree symbolized both success and eternal life. The myrtle tree is one of the four blessed plants used in the Jewish festival of Tabernacles (Sukkoth), a Jewish fall festival. To meet the requirement for Sukkoth, three myrtle leaves must emerge from the myrtle stem at one point. Note: The Bible myrtle tree is not our American crape myrtle.

Growing New Testament Parable Plants

Wheat

Ancient Israelites planted winter wheat (*Triticum aestivum*) in October to November and harvested it about May. In the United States, 70 to 80 percent of wheat comes from farmers growing winter wheat. Winter wheat needs about 180 to 250 days to mature. It requires a cold period of chilling (vernalization)—down to 20 degrees Fahrenheit during the early growth period. As you would expect, winter wheat tolerates frost in early stages; however, in the active growth stage (in the spring), frost can damage head development and flower formation. Wheat is moderately tolerant of saline in the soil, but high levels of salt in soil can decrease wheat yield. The optimal Plant Zones for winter wheat are 6 to 8.

Winter wheat grows best in full sun and in a wide range of soils, but medium textured soil (loam and sandy loam) is preferred. The optimal soil pH is from 6 to 8. Winter wheat is largely a rain-fed crop in temperate climates. When the wheat head is flowering, wheat needs water. In spring if rainfall is low, wheat benefits from irrigation. Generally, farmers allow about 60 percent of soil water to be used before soil is irrigated. For an excellent yield of wheat, farmers add nitrogen, phosphorous, and potassium to their soil.

Wheat stalks grows up to four feet and shouldn't be pruned. The grain head is about five inches long and looks bushy because hair-like structures cover wheat kernels. Grain heads were threshed, then winnowed to remove chaff (hair structures, stalks). The first president of the United States and avid farmer, George Washington said that a farmer who doesn't save and replant his own seeds was in effect a poor farmer.

Most gardeners don't grow wheat and most assuredly they don't thresh wheat; however, gardeners who plant a Bible garden can plant several rows of wheat for demonstration purposes. Last year I planted wheat in our church garden for the first time. It was a learning experience; primarily I learned that five to six shorter rows were more impressive to view than two longer rows. Further, in my Plant Zone 7, planting winter wheat is likely a better option than planting spring wheat.

Darnel

Darnel (*Lolium temulentum*), known as weeds, tares, or poison ryegrass, probably originated in the Mediterranean Basin. Darnel is widely naturalized in subtropics and temperate regions of many countries in the world. Generally, darnel plants grow in the same climate and Plant Zones (6 to 8) as wheat; however, they will grow in deserts to include extreme deserts. Darnel has invaded most of the United States to include Alaska.

Darnel grows best in full sun and won't grow in shade. This weed isn't particular about type of soil, but flourishes when soil is somewhat moist. Because darnel is an invasive species that often spreads as a contaminant of wheat, it is almost never planted deliberately. Farmers and gardeners don't fertilize, irrigate, or prune darnel.

Darnel stalks grow to thirty to thirty-six inches with leaves that alternate side to side. Stalks have a six- to ten-inch head. Initially, stalks, leaves, and flowers are green. Flowers bloom late spring. As darnel matures, the plant turns black. This black color is a sure way to differentiate darnel from wheat, which as a cream or golden color.

Flowers are bisexual and are pollinated by the wind. Flowers turn into seeds. Darnel is an annual plant. It regrows when seeds fall into the soil and germinate the next year. The darnel seed itself isn't poisonous, but seeds are frequently contaminated by a poisonous fungus. The fungus can cause hallucinations and central nervous system damage in man.

Anemones

The lily of the field in Jesus's Sermon on the Mount was a field flower. Most botanists believe the wildflower was the anemone (*Anemone coronaria*), known as the windflower. Anemones grow throughout Israel from the heights of Mount Hermon to the extreme deserts in southern Israel. They also grow along the Mediterranean Sea coastline. Windflowers grow in high mountain valleys under deciduous trees. They go into dormancy about mid-summer. Generally, anemones grow in Plant Zones 3 to 9, but seem to grow best in Zones 6 to 9. To find anemone flowers in the Roanoke Valley, I had to visit several nurseries. Few nurseries sold them.

Anemones grow in both full sun and partial shade. I planted them in a garden area that receives afternoon sun. Possibly, if they were planted in an area that received full sun, they would have bloomed early in the season. Some anemone cultivars begin to grow in late winter (February) and bloom in early spring. Anemones aren't picky about type of soil except they demand well-drained, but not soggy, soil. As the number of hours of direct sunlight increases, so does the anemone's need for additional water. I use a soaker hose to water the area where anemone are planted in the church Bible garden. Normally, I water two to three times a week during dry summer weather.

Whether anemones are grown in containers or in a garden, fertilizer is a good idea. You can use organic materials such as peat moss, compost, or decomposed manure; all work well and are widely available. My anemones grow to about two feet tall. Flowers stay on the stems for about a week then petals begin to drop. Depending on the cultivar purchased, the flower stem may not be straight; some stems seem to form an S shape near the top. Nurseries sell double-bloom anemone which have more petals than the traditional anemone flower.

Anemone flowers are bisexual. They produce no nectar, but insects (beetles, bees) feed on the pollen. The flower self pollinates and is pollinated by wind and insects. The fruit is a small one-seeded fruit (achne). Seeds have fluffy hairs which aid wind dispersion. Perhaps anemones grow from seeds, but not in my garden. After three years of trying to grow them from seeds, I bought small plants. If you purchase bulbs, soak them a few hours in lukewarm water before planting them in soil. Then, plant bulbs about one to two inches deep. Don't worry about which side of the bulb is face up; regardless of how you position the bulb, they will grow.

Mustard Trees

The mustard tree (*Salvadora persica*) is an evergreen shrub or small tree, often referred to as the toothbrush tree. Most likely, it originated in Persia (Iran). Other places where the tree grows naturally are north and east Africa. Mustard trees grow best in hot, dry climates. Both saline and drought-tolerant, mustard trees are found on sand dunes as well as around water holes. Mustard trees don't grow well in humid climates. When humidity is consistently high, tree growth is stunted and trees develop mold. Mustard trees grow best where precipitation varies between twelve and forty inches. In the United States, trees are found in Plant Zones 7 to 11.

Trees grow best in full sun. The mustard tree has adapted to alkaline and saline soils, but will grow in soil without salt. Because toothbrush trees leach salt from the soil, it has potential to reclaim saline soils. It is one of the few trees that prefers clay soil, but will grow in loamy black soil and sand. Generally, the tree doesn't grow at altitudes greater than 5,900 feet.

Slow growing mustard trees can reach a height of twenty feet. Often they appear as wide as tall. Trees are many-branched and branches start to grow low to ground; the trunk is short.

For these reasons, mustard trees are often used as hedges. When grown as a hedge, trees need to be pruned into the desired shape. Rarely is the tree fertilized; however, like any tree, the mustard tree benefits from a general-purpose fertilizer applied annually in the spring before growth starts.

Leaves start out light green but turn dark green as the tree ages. Flowers, green and yellow, grow on long tendrils; they are bisexual and are pollinated by the wind and insects. The fruit is pea-sized and round. When fruit is dried, as it is in the Punjab area of India, it is sweet and reminiscent of a current. The fruit turns into a seed with a pulp around it. Before planting a seed, remove the pulp. Only after the pulp is removed is the actual tiny size of the seed appreciated. Mustard tree seeds are one of the smallest seeds in the world. Often mustard tree seeds are considered a spice.

The short stems of the *Salvadora persica* can be harvested for toothbrushes. Roots are made into a pain-relieving salve. In Africa and the Middle East, farmers use mustard trees for livestock shade. Animals feed on tree shoots. Many books on Bible plants list the mustard plant as the black mustard plant (*Brassica nigra*). The black mustard plant, although green, leafy, and attractive, isn't the mustard tree named in Jesus's parable.

Mulberry Trees

In the Bible, the mulberry tree (*Morus nigra*) is also named the sycamine tree. Most likely, black mulberry trees originated in Persia (Iran). In the United States, mulberry trees grow in Plant Zones 5 to 9. Trees grow best where summers are long and hot. The black mulberry tree is deciduous; it drops its leaves in the fall and grows new ones in the spring.

Black mulberry trees grow in full sun or semi-shade. Because they tolerate atmospheric pollution, they can be grown in urban environments, assuming there is a plan to deal with the tree's fruit when it drops onto sidewalks or green space. Where external temperature is hot, trees grow more rapidly. The black mulberry tree is one of the least particular trees in nature. It grows in sand, loam, and clay soils. The soil pH can be acidic, neutral, or alkaline; however, black mulberry trees do best in acidic soil (pH 5.6 to 6.5).

Water requirements are average; however, overwatering can lead to wilted leaves. Black mulberry trees prefer well-drained soil. In the kibbutz where we stayed in southern Israel, residents watered the mulberry tree. Black mulberry trees seem to produce an inordinate number of limbs and leaves. Often leaves obscure the mulberries. If you like to see individual limbs on trees, you may want to prune your mulberry tree; however, pruning isn't necessary. A spring application of a good fertilizer is a good idea. The tree's flowers appear only after all danger of frost is over. Flowers grow in short, green, relatively nondescript catkins (shaped like a cat tail). Often they appear in short clusters. After pollination, female flowers ripen into one-inch, blackberry-shaped edible fruits. One plant book reported that black mulberries can grow up to three inches long; however, I have never seen one that large. Ultimately, the berry becomes succulent, fat, and full of juice. As expected the black mulberry tree's berries are black.

My personal experience with mulberry trees is that the tree is "dirty," for want of a better word. We had a prolific mulberry tree where I was reared in southern Pennsylvania. Every summer the tree dropped giant, juicy berries onto the lawn. It was hard to play on that side of the house because fruit covered the ground. Also, the juice tended to stain playing children's clothes.

Israeli Giant Reeds

The Israeli giant reed (*Arundo donax*) is known as the Cypress cane. The reed is native to countries surrounding the Mediterranean Sea. The Israeli reed isn't native to the United States, but has been widely planted in the southern half of the country, i.e., Plant

Zones 6 to 10. Although the reed is most often planted as an ornamental, in southeastern United States it has been planted along ditches for erosion control. In California, giant reeds escaped cultivation. They are prolific growers in streams, ditches, seeps, and even on lower hills.

The Israeli reed prefers full sun and will die if planted in full shade. The Israeli giant reed tolerates a wide variety of ecological conditions and flourishes in all types of soil from heavy clays to loose sands and gravelly soils. At one time, botanists thought the giant reed couldn't tolerate salt and maritime exposure; however, giant reeds grow on sand dunes near Israeli seashores such as the Sharon Plain. In a temperate climate, altitude doesn't seem to be an important factor in reed growth, but don't expect reeds to grow in mountains or high mountain valleys. Generally, the giant reed doesn't grow in states north of Indiana.

Textbooks claim that ideal growth conditions are well-drained soils with abundant moisture. During its first year of growth, the Israeli reed can be set back by lack of moisture; however, once the reed is two-to-three years old, it can survive drought conditions. I bought seedlings and planted them along the side of the church where water runs off the roof. Rainfall this summer in the Roanoke Valley was higher than normal. I didn't water or irrigate the reeds. They grew beautifully and stood proudly until mid-November. Then, I cut them down for the winter; this spring they are re-growing.

The giant reed tolerates strong winds. The Israeli reed is one of the largest grasses and grows to twenty feet tall. Generally, they are green, but the ones I purchased last year were variegated green and white. Don't prune the reed midseason even though it appears to grow very tall. If you do, you will miss out on the large flowers that grow on plumelike panicles at the top of the reed. Time of bloom varies with heat and sun with textbooks noting that bloom time is March through September. In our temperate climate, the reeds at the church flowered September through October.

Israeli reeds growing in nature aren't fertilized; however, we gardeners want to fertilize all plants. Probably, an annual general-purpose fertilizer applied after the last frost will encourage reed growth. Although I didn't prune the reeds in our garden, I had to stake them with a six-foot-tall sturdy stake. They wanted to bend forward toward the afternoon sun.

Some notable universities reported that the Israeli giant reed doesn't produce viable seeds. Generally, reed replication occurs by roots (rhizomes) sprouting and spreading. I purchased six reed shoots from a mail-order nursery last spring and planted them. They all grew beautifully and came back up in the spring. Because Roanoke winters can drop to less than zero degrees Fahrenheit at night, in late autumn we mulched around the reed base with wheat straw.

Carob Trees

The carob tree is the *Ceratonia siliqua*. Carob trees grow best where summers are hot and winters are cool. Mature trees can endure a wide variation of temperatures, from 20 degrees to 122 degrees Fahrenheit. Frost during blooming season prevents flowers from blooming and fruit from setting on trees. Young branches exposed to severe winds can be damaged by sea salt. For carob trees, the optimal Plant Zones is 9 to 11 so I have not attempted to grow them in Roanoke (Plant Zone 7). Carob trees thrive in full sun or very light shade.

Carob trees are identified as drought-tolerant. Ideal annual precipitation is thirty inches, but trees will thrive on less rain. In the United States, carob trees grow in dry areas of California, Arizona, and Texas; both Florida and Hawaii will sustain carob tree growth as long as plants don't stand in water. Irrigation isn't necessary, unless the season is very dry. Then, irrigate deeply every three to four weeks. After carob pods have turned brown, don't allow them to be exposed to heavy dew or rain. Wet pods will ferment quickly.

In Israel, carob trees grow at altitudes of 1,312 feet, but carob trees could originated in the mountains of Yemen, which are taller. Carob trees flourish in widely divergent soil, from rocky hillsides to deep sand to heavy loam. Trees don't tolerate acidic or wet soils, nor do trees grow near coastlines. Soil pH must be alkaline. Usually, home growers don't fertilize carob trees; however, on carob plantations, some growers fertilize annually to promote growth. Prune to remove dead or diseased branches about twice per year. For some reason, rats climb carob trees and gnaw tree bark until branches die.

Generally, gardeners must plant one male carob tree for every twenty-five to thirty female trees to ensure fertilization of flowers. Growers can graft a male flower branch onto a female flower tree rather than interplant male trees. Before planting, dried hard carob seeds need to be scarified or chipped. Then, soak seeds in water until they swell. Germination rates are about 25 percent; consequently, often young whips (seedlings) are purchased and planted. Carob trees begin to bear fruit about the sixth year after planting. Flowers emit an unpleasant and strong odor that draws insects. The fruit is the carob pod which must be harvested before winter rains. Trees may produce for eighty to one hundred years.

Carob is a substitute for chocolate but has no caffeine. In the Mediterranean region, peasants have lived on carob pods during famines. In ancient times, Middle East merchants weighed gold and gemstones against the seeds of a carob tree, thus the origin of the word "carat," a measure of weight for gems and precious metals. Carob pods are eaten during the Jewish celebration of Tu B'Shevat, a holiday known as the New Year of the Trees. Celebrated on the fifteenth day of the Jewish month of Shevat, Tu B'Shevat is the new year for the purpose of calculating the age of trees for tithing (Leviticus. 19:23–25).

Olive Trees

The olive tree (*Olea europaea*) was domesticated around 4000 BC. It originated in the eastern Mediterranean Basin, possibly in Israel and Syria. Primarily, olive trees grow in Plant Zones 8 to 10 in the United States. Often trees will be damaged by temperatures below 17 degrees Fahrenheit and most won't survive if external temperature is below 10 degrees Fahrenheit. Some newer varieties of olive trees are tougher and are more likely to make it through colder spells. If you live in Zone 7, *Olea europaea* Mission or Arbequina cultivars are more likely to survive winter temperatures. Even with these more hardy cultivars, the tree will benefit from using wheat or pine straw as high as ten inches up the base of the tree for at least the first five years of its life. I've investigated white fabric covers (often called row covers) to protect olive trees in the winter; however, often these covers only protect to about 24 degrees Fahrenheit. Our valley winters see temperatures down to 0 to 5 degrees on the coldest nights. To be safe, if you live in any Plant Zone lower than 8, grow olives trees in a container and take them inside in the fall. In the spirit of complete transparency, the olive trees I planted last summer don't look like they made it through the winter.

The dry composition of the olive tree makes them fairly drought-tolerant. Often olive trees thrive on hillsides where water drainage is better than in the valleys. Although the olive tree isn't massive like the aloe tree, it can grow to sixty-five feet tall. Spreading branches form a dense canopy. Gardeners need to carefully select the plant site because of these growth patterns. Amazingly, olive trees can live up to one thousand years which means that some of the olive trees in the Garden of Gethsemane and on the Mount of Olives may be only two or three generations away from those that grew in these areas when Jesus walked there.

Olive trees prefer to grow in full sun and need a minimum of six hours of full sunlight each day. Soil can be sand or loam. Just because the olive tree tolerates drought doesn't mean it is a desert plant. In order to thrive, olive trees need water, particularly if the soil is sand that doesn't retain water. Drip irrigation (soaker hose) is of little or no use in sandy soils. If your soil is sand, the best way to irrigate is low-volume spray irrigation.

Many growers tell you that olive trees don't need fertilizer; however, trees benefit from yearly fertilization. Olive Tree Growers[4] include the following suggestions for olive tree growth: (a) avoid heavy applications of a fast release fertilizer because it can damage plants and leach into ground water, (b) don't fertilize before mid-March (unless you live in a very warm climate) or after mid-August, and (c) water well after fertilizing.

For the most part, olive trees don't need to be pruned to produce olives. When you can prune an olive tree to obtain a desirable shape, remember that fruit is produced on branches that grew the previous spring or summer. If you cut them off, you will lessen olive production. Very old olive trees are hollow, secondary to fungus infection that attacks the wood; consequently, as trees age, some pruning may become necessary.

Generally, new olive trees grow from stem cuttings rather than from seed. Often young trees must be staked for support when moved from a pot to the outside. As the tree grows, a heavier stake may become necessary particularly when winds are common. Use arborist's tape to attach the tree to the stake.

Oleaster Trees

The wild olive tree (*Elaeagnus angustifolia*) is called the oleaster and Russian olive. The wild olive is native to the northeastern area of the Near East, most likely at the borders of Syria and Turkey. From these areas, oleaster spread throughout the Mediterranean Basin. Wild olive trees date back to the New Stone Age (beginning 10,000 BC). In the United States, wild olive trees grow in

Plant Zones 3 to 8, often thriving along riverbanks and streams. The tree isn't frost tender.

Wild olive trees grow best in full sun. Although trees can't grow in full shade, they grow in dappled shade such as on the edge of woodlands. Wild olive trees grow on hills and mountains up to nine thousand feet or more. They develop a deep taproot as well as lateral roots. Ideally, they are planted and left to grow in place.

Wild olive trees grow in all types of soil, i.e., sand, loam, and clay, and in soils with variable pH (acidic, neutral, and alkaline) to include saline soils along seashores. The wild olive tree fixes, or uses, atmospheric nitrogen to promote growth of roots, branches, etc.; consequently, wild olive trees don't deprive the soil of this nutrient. Wild olive trees are drought-tolerant and indifferent to wind and heat. They have adapted to dry or moist soil as long as the soil is well-drained. The wild olive tree can grow in nutrition-ally poor soils and rarely needs to be fertilized.

Typically, the wild olive tree grows to twenty feet tall and it has a wide canopy. Trunks are multibranched and may resprout after being cut down. Brown bark constantly sheds (exfoliates), similar to our common river birch. Branches tend to droop. In the United Kingdom, wild olive trees are pruned into high hedges. *Angustifolia* means narrow-leaved and indeed the tree leaf is thin, similar to a willow leaf. The current year's twigs are thin, gray, and may have thorns. Although classified as a deciduous tree, wild olive tree leaves don't change color in the fall. Trees hold leaves until late autumn.

Flowers contain both male and female organs and bees are the primary pollinator. Seeds can take up to eighteen months to germinate. Sometimes trees are propagated by layering; however, more often gardeners buy and plant cuttings. Be very careful when purchasing cuttings. Often, tree cuttings haven't been rooted and allowed to grow adequately before being sold. Recently, I purchased six seedlings from a reputable nursery. All died, despite regular care and tending. One expert recommends that growers plant cuttings and allow them to grow two to three years before selling them. Mulching around the tree with pine or wheat straw will increase the odds of trees remaining alive over winter months.

The oval wild olive fruit is about one-half inch long and contains a single seed. It tastes dry, sweet, and mealy. Unlike domesticated olives which are often eaten green, wild olive fruit should be fully ripe before eating. Even slightly underripe wild olives have an astringent taste. The main difference between wild and cultivated olive trees is the big and juicier fruits of cultivated trees.

Buckthorn Trees

The Mediterranean buckthorn (*Rhamnus lycioides*) is the Palestinian buckthorn, sometime named the black hawthorn. Its origin is the Mediterranean Basin, i.e., western Middle East, southern Europe, and northern Africa. Despite the buckthorn being a Mediterranean Basin tree, it can endure below zero degrees Fahrenheit temperatures. Although adult bushes or trees can withstand high winds, young plants benefit from long, solid stakes if winds are high. In high-wind areas, stake buckthorns for the first three to four years. The buckthorn grows in shrublands, woodlands, and on mountains; however, it isn't seen in desert areas where precipitation is less than eight inches annually. The Mediterranean buckthorn grows in bright places with direct sunlight. It won't grow in the shade.

In the Mediterranean Basin, particularly Israel, the buckthorn grows three-to-six feet tall; however, in temperate climates with more rainfall, buckthorn will grow to forty feet and become a tree. Buckthorn plants aren't particular about soil. They grow in sand, loam, and clay as well as stony soil. Similarly, buckthorn is indifferent to soil pH. Buckthorns seem to grow equally well in either dry or moist soil as long as soil is well-drained. If rainfall is extremely scarce, buckthorn benefit from five-to-ten gallons of water every four-to-five weeks.

For optimal growth, buckthorn trees can be fertilized when the tree is planted and every two-to-three years thereafter. Annual fertilization isn't necessary; however, if you elect to fertilize, the best time to apply fertilizer is spring immediately after growth starts. Organic fertilizer from mature manure is optimal. Gardeners may decide to prune trees to manage their size. Prune during the late fall or early winter in most temperate climates.

Flowers are bisexual and generally are pollinated by insects. Often the flower aroma is described as sweet. Fruit is an oval berry less than one-half inch in size. The inside of the berry contains a seed. When ripe, berries are black. Although buckthorn plants will grow from seeds, the process is arduous. Gardeners will do better to purchase seedlings from a nursery.

Field Grass

Orchard grass (*Dactylis glomerata*) originated in the Mediterranean Basin area where summers are long and hot. The grass was introduced into the United States and now grows in all fifty states; it is particularly adapted to Plant Zones 4 to 8. This deeply rooted grass grows in dense clumps and is useful to check soil erosion. Often it is found in disturbed areas. When our church was constructed, the contractor pushed concrete, stone, etc., to one area on the property. Orchard grass grows well there and looks attractive most of the year. If you plant orchard grass close together, it will form a perennial ground cover.

Orchard grass grows in full sun and in light woodlands (semi-shade). It grows under most trees and will grow at altitudes from sea level to 13,100 feet. Orchard grass is drought-tolerant and prefers annual precipitation of between twelve and sixty-nine inches. It grows successfully in sandy and loamy soil. Orchard grass will grow in heavy clay soil as long as the soil is well-drained. Soil pH can be very acidic to very basic (alkaline) and orchard grass will still thrive. For the most part, orchard grass doesn't have to be fertilized; however, I fertilize almost everything in early spring so my orchard grass gets fertilizer at that time as well.

Orchard grass is only occasionally grown for lawns because grass blades are so coarse. Alternatively, if you have heavy shade areas at your church or home, you may want to try planting orchard grass there. Grass grows up to three feet tall. If you are using the clumps for accent, you don't have to cut it. Orchard grass starts growing early in the year and blooms by late spring. Initially flower heads (panicles) are green, but in full sun they may develop a red tinge. As heads mature, seeds become a gray-brown. Flowers have both male and female organs and are pollinated by wind. Seeds attract birds.

Orchard grass clumps can be purchased at most nurseries or you can plant seeds. If you plant seeds, put five-to-six seeds in each spot. It is easier to remove excess growth than to not have planted enough seed. Seeds germinate in three weeks. Whether you purchase your orchard grass or decide to use seeds, plant them in the spring. Ideally, orchard grass is planted where you want them to grow.

Originally, farmers imported orchard grass for grazing livestock and to cut for winter fodder. I've not noticed that deer eat orchard grass although they seem to nibble on almost everything else in the garden.

Wormwood

Over two hundred types of artemisia have been named; however, the wormwood of the Bible is the *Artemisia absinthium*, also called the common artemisia. Although wormwood's origins are North Africa and temperate areas of Eurasia, the herbaceous plant grows in United States Plant Zones 4 to 9. I've planted several types of artemisia in our church Bible garden to include

Artemisia absinthium. For the most part, they receive late afternoon sun. Artemisia grows up to three feet tall and spreads laterally the same distance. Stems are firm and at the base look woody. Leaves are gray-green (silver-green) and divide into segments, becoming smaller as they move from the bottom to top of plants. Stems and leaves are covered with fine white silky hairs.

Artemisia grows in poor to moderately fertile soil, such as clay-loam. Good soil drainage is a requirement for growth. The plant doesn't grow well in moist or wet soil; roots are susceptible to root rot. Generally, foliage declines where summer rainfall or humidity is high, as in the southeastern United States. If foliage declines or stems flop over, wormwood can be revitalized by shearing it. Wormwood doesn't need to be watered unless rainfall doesn't occur for about four-to-six weeks. When watering, water deeply.

Gardeners can prune mature plants if they appear leggy, i.e., you see more stem than leaves. Normally, wormwood should look leafy. Often artemisia is named "silver mound" because it grows in clumps and has a silver hue. On artemisia plants, flowers appear in the summer. They are small, round, pale yellow, and bisexual. Wind pollination occurs. Unless you want artemisia to spread, promptly deadhead the flowers to prevent self-seeding. Artemisia will grow from cuttings. In late fall, I cut artemisia down to soil level; it regrows in the spring.

Some texts identified that wormwood leaves and roots exude a substance that restricts the growth of many neighboring plants. This may be true because over several years, I've seen no other herbs grow near wormwood, not even mint, which once planted seems to grow every which way. Because of their acidic odor, leaves are used as insect and moth repellants.

Absinthium means "without sweetness" and refers to the extremely bitter taste of the plant juices. In 2007, a 1912 ban on using absinthe in the United States was overturned. Natural *Artemisia absinthium* is now used in alcoholic drinks.

References

1. Modzelevich, Martha. *Flowers in Israel.* http://www.flowersinisrael.com, 2016.

2. Dirr, Michael A. *Manual of woody landscape plants.* Champaign, IL: Stipes Publishing LLC, 2009.

3. Sibley, David Allen. *The Sibley guide to trees.* New York, NY: Knopf, Inc., 2009.

4. Olive Tree Growers. http://olivetreegrowers.com/, 2016.

Index Table of Plants

Location OT = Old Testament NT = New Testament	Parable Name	Plant Names Common Name (Taxonomy Name)
OT: Numbers 24:1-9	Balaam's Parable of the Aloe Trees	Aloe Tree (*Aquilaria malaccensis*)
OT: Judges 9	Trees Crown a King	Thorn Tree or Thornbush (*Ziziphus spina-christi*)
OT: 2 Chronicles 25:17-18	The Thistle and the Cedar	Spotted Golden Thistle (*Scolymus maculatus*) Cedar Tree (*Cedrus libani*)
OT: Psalm 37	Transient Plants and Wicked Men	Laurel Tree (*Laurus nobilis*)
OT: Psalm 80:8-13; Isaiah 5:1-6	Parables of Vineyards	Grape (*Vitis vinifera*)
OT: Ecclesiastes 7:6	Crackling Thorns and Laughter of Fools	Thorny Burnet (*Sarcopoterium spinosum*)
OT: Isaiah 28:24-29	Poem of a Plowman	Cumin (*Cuminum cyminum*) Barley (*Hordeum vulgare*)
OT: Jeremiah 1:11-12	Vision of an Almond Branch	Almond Tree (*Prunus dulcis* also called *P.amygdalus*)
OT: Jeremiah 24	Two Baskets of Figs	Figs (*Ficus carica*)
OT: Ezekiel 4	Parable of Famine Bread	Broad Beans (*Vicia faba*)
OT: Hosea 14:8	God as an Evergreen Tree	Cypress Tree (*Cupressus sempervirens*)

OT: Zechariah 1:8-13	Among the Myrtle Trees	Myrtle Tree (*Myrtus communis*)
NT: Matthew 3:12	John the Baptist and Winnowing Wheat	Wheat (*Triticum aestivum*)
NT: Matthew 13:24-30, 36-43	Harvesting Weeds (Darnel)	Darnel or Weeds (*Lolium temulentum*)
NT: Matthew 6:28-30	Lily of the Field	Lily of the Field (*Anemone coronaria*)
NT: Mark 4:30-32	Growth of a Mustard Seed	Mustard Tree (*Salvadora persica*)
NT: Luke 17:6	Moving a Mulberry Tree	Mulberry Tree (*Morus nigra*)
NT: Luke 7:18-28	Reeds Shaken by the Wind	Israeli Reed (*Arundo donax*)
NT: Luke 15:11-32	Lost Son and Carob Pods	Carob Tree (*Ceratonia siliqua*)
NT: Matthew 25:1-13	Virgins with Oil Lamps	Olive Tree (*Olea europaea*)
NT: Romans 11:16-24	In-grafted Wild Olive Branch	Wild Olive Tree (*Elaeagnus angustifolia*)
NT: Hebrews 6:7-8	Productive versus Thorn-Infested Land	Buckthorn (*Rhamnus lycioides*)
NT: 1 Peter 1:23-26	Grass in the Field	Orchard Grass (*Dactylis glomerata*)
NT: Revelation 8:10-11	Wormwood, a Shooting Star	Wormwood (*Artemisia absinthium*)

listen|imagine|view|experience

AUDIO BOOK DOWNLOAD INCLUDED WITH THIS BOOK!

In your hands you hold a complete digital entertainment package. In addition to the paper version, you receive a free download of the audio version of this book. Simply use the code listed below when visiting our website. Once downloaded to your computer, you can listen to the book through your computer's speakers, burn it to an audio CD or save the file to your portable music device (such as Apple's popular iPod) and listen on the go!

How to get your free audio book digital download:

1. Visit www.tatepublishing.com and click on the e|LIVE logo on the home page.
2. Enter the following coupon code:
   933b-9909-d5c4-fcc2-eb0e-f8b2-d9d7-c02d
3. Download the audio book from your e|LIVE digital locker and begin enjoying your new digital entertainment package today!

CPSIA information can be obtained
at www.ICGtesting.com
Printed in the USA
BVOW07s1207071016
464161BV00010B/3/P

9 781683 522706